The
New
Believers

The New Believers

Young
Religion
in
America

by Daniel Cohen

M. Evans and Company, Inc./New York, N. Y. 10017

M. Evans and Company titles are distributed in
the United States by the J. B. Lippincott Company,
East Washington Square, Philadelphia, Pa. 19105;
and in Canada by McClelland & Stewart Ltd.,
25 Hollinger Road, Toronto M4B 3G2, Ontario

Library of Congress Cataloging in Publication Data

Cohen, Daniel.
  The new believers.

  Bibliography: p.
  Includes index.
  1. United States—Religion. 2. Sects—United States. I. Title.
BR516.5.C63   200'.973   74-28087
ISBN 0-87131-174-7

4.61   12-15-75

To Jered, Jethro, Joab, Julie,
Mercedes, Amos, Gavin, Yvonne,
and all the others that I met
who have dared to be different

Acknowledgments

Practically all of the religious groups that I contacted during the course of my research for this book were extremely cooperative and generous with both information and pictures. I would particularly like to thank: Jered and Ammi of the Children of God; Connie Best and Julie Cooper of the Divine Light Mission; Witches Gavin Frost and Dr. Leo Louis Martello; Mother Mercedes, Father Joab and Brother Amos of the Foundation; and Ruth Gullixson of Subud.

Contents

The Other Believers   11

Section I   The New Christians
The Children of God   21
The Jesus People   41
The Charismatic Revival Movement   53
The Unification Church   63

Section II   Eastern Religions
The Divine Light Mission   77
Transcendental Meditation   95
Hare Krishna   105
Subud   117

Section III   The Occult
Witchcraft   127
Satanism   145
The Process/The Foundation   158

Conclusion   175
For Further Information   179
Bibliography   183
Index   187

PHOTO CREDITS

PAGE

Title page	Associated Press
18	David Wilson
29	David Wilson
37	Daniel Cohen
47	Religious News Service
57	Religious News Service
60	Religious News Service
69	Religious News Service
87	United Press International
99	Religious News Service
107	Associated Press
111	Associated Press
124	Holt, Rinehart and Winston
151	Dodd Mead

The Other Believers

There has been a good deal of talk in recent years about the growth of new and often strange religions among the youth of America. Some people have viewed this development with great alarm, seeing it as a sign of the decline of the traditional organized religions and the values that they represent, or as a rejection of rationalism and a scientific outlook. The sight of college students dabbling in witchcraft really upsets a lot of people.

Others look at the development from an optimistic point of view. They see the growth of religious movements among the young, no matter how bizarre these movements may seem, as a sign that this generation has turned its back on gross materialism and is groping for new spiritual values. A few enthusiasts have gone so far as to proclaim that the United States has entered a period of a great religious awakening. They say that the Age of Aquarius, an age of new spirituality, has begun.

Perhaps so. It certainly seems as though there are many more religious movements now than there were just a few years ago. But what many people fail to recall, or perhaps never knew, is that America has always been the home of highly unorthodox religious movements.

The Puritans who came to Massachusetts were regarded as religious fanatics by the Anglican majority of their native England. The Quakers who settled in Pennsylvania were fiercely persecuted in Europe because of their religious beliefs.

The New World was a magnet for oppressed religious minorities from all parts of the Old World. There were the Amish, the Hutterites, the Rappites, the Inspirationists and many, many others. Some of these groups lived communally, as do many of the Jesus People today. Communal Christian religious groups past and present all point to the same passages in the Book of Acts to prove, by Scripture, that the early Christians also lived a communal life.

The Shakers were a highly successful communal sect that developed in America at about the time of the American Revolution and flourished until the end of the nineteenth century. There are still a few elderly Shakers left alive, but the sect will clearly be extinct within a few years. The Shakers believed that total avoidance of all sexual relations was the only way to follow God's plan.

On the other hand, John Humphrey Noyes, an ordained minister and devout, albeit unorthodox, Christian, believed that God's plan called for free love. Noyes founded the Oneida community where he practiced what he preached for a quarter of a century. The community finally collapsed when Noyes fled the country for fear of being imprisoned in 1876.

The first great westward migration in the history of America was made by the Mormons, a religious sect born in the visions of a New York State farm boy. The doctrines of Joseph Smith, founder and prophet of the Mormons, were as strange and shocking to the people of the early nineteenth century as the doctrines of someone like the Guru Maharaj Ji are to people today. Guru Maharaj Ji got hit in the face with a pie in Detroit, but a mob in Illinois shot Joseph Smith. Mary Baker Eddy, the founder of Christian Science, was denounced as a crook and a lunatic when she first propounded her doctrine that there is no such thing as disease.

Yet despite violence, denunciation and ridicule both Mormonism and Christian Science have not only survived, they have prospered. Today both are recognized and respectable religions. Indeed, both are noted for their basically conservative appeal.

Jehovah's Witnesses is another uniquely American religious creation. It is today one of the fastest growing religions in the world, and while it is not considered quite respectable yet by more conventional Protestants, Jehovah's Witnesses is well on its way to becoming so, simply because it has been around long enough, and people have gotten used to it.

Many of today's unorthodox religions are profoundly apocalyptic—that is, they predict that the world is going to come to an end soon, probably before the year 2000. The apocalyptic view is such a common feature of these religions that after a while one begins to get the uncomfortable feeling that perhaps they know something that the rest of us don't. But apocalyptic sects are not new in America either. Back in 1844 thousands of followers of a preacher named William Miller climbed to hilltops on October 22 and waited for the world to end, as their prophet had predicted. The world didn't end, though Miller's movement did.

Not all unorthodox religion in America has been an outgrowth of Christianity. Spiritualism, a movement which holds that certain individuals called mediums can talk to the spirits of the dead, began in upstate New York in 1848. Today spiritualism is a worldwide phenomena.

Surely few religions have appeared more unorthodox than Theosophy, a system of beliefs propounded by Madame Helena Petrovena Blavatsky, a colorful Russian adventuress. Madame Blavatsky was aided by Colonel William P. Olcott, an American, and the whole idea was born in an apartment on the West Side of Manhattan.

It is difficult to explain Theosophy briefly, for its doctrines are complex and, to the outsider at least, often contradictory. Theosophy was heavily influenced by the Hindu religion, and stresses reincarnation and the "evolution" of the soul through different "planes of existence." But an equal influence on Theosophy was occultism. The word "occult" means hidden or secret, and Theosophy holds that there is a body of secret knowledge passed down through the ages by a select body of "masters" or "adepts." Madame Blavatsky contended that she was in touch with a band of semidivine "Ascended Masters" or "Mahatmas" who lived in the mountains of Tibet.

Today there are still thousands of Theosophists in the United States, though the movement has been fragmented by numerous internal disputes.

There certainly has been an increasing interest in Eastern religions in America over the past twenty years, but as far back as 1893 Swami Vivenkananda visited America and founded the Vedanta Society, which still has a small but influential following.

Vedanta is a religious philosophy based on the Vedas, the ancient scriptures of India. Vedanta teaches that all of the great religions can be harmonized, since each in its own way adores God; and that the aim of man on earth is to discover his own true nature, which is also a realization of the nature of God. This realization can be reached by many routes: meditation, prayer, yoga or doing service for others.

I am not trying to contend that the current popularity of unorthodox religions is no greater or more significant now than it has been in the past. While living through a historical event, there is really no way of judging whether it represents a major turning point or a minor footnote in history. I am merely trying to place the subject in perspective.

Unorthodox religions are nothing new on the American scene. Religious controversy is nothing new either. All of the religious groups that we are going to look at in this book are extremely controversial. Charges ranging from madness to fraud have been brought against them. We are going to examine these charges as fully as possible. But it is extremely important to keep in mind that similar charges have been raised against all unorthodox or minority religions.

We should also try to remember that the member of an unorthodox religion often has a very different way of looking at things than the outsider. We may feel that the leader of a particular sect acts in an arbitrary and dictatorial manner. His followers, however, might well feel that the leader is expressing the Divine Will, or is himself divine. Thus, they are not following orders, they are acting in conformity with the Will of God. Over and over the members of different groups stressed to me that the "freedom" of the outside world was an illusion, but by following the orders and rules of their group they had attained a "greater freedom." You do not have to agree with this, but you should try to understand it.

Even after the subject is placed in some perspective there can be little doubt that unorthodox religions are flourishing in the U.S. today, and that their appeal is particularly strong among the young.

It would be hopeless to try to cover all the unorthodox religious movements currently popular in the U.S. There are simply too many of them for a book of this size. It is even difficult to try and define which religions are unorthodox, or are really religions in the first place. I have divided the subject into three general headings— Christian, Eastern and Occult—and have tried to examine some of the largest or most influential groups in each of these general classifications. In the end, though, the choice of what has been covered and what has not is a highly personal one.

A notable omission is the Church of Scientology, a bizarre healing-type cult that was created by an ex-science fiction author named L. Ron Hubbard. The group claims to have many hundreds of thousands of members, and while that may be something of an exaggeration, there is no doubt that Scientology is both large and influential. But Scientology in one form or another has been around for over twenty years, and has been covered extensively elsewhere.

There is nothing in this book about spiritualism, Bahai or other unorthodox religions that have also been established in America for a long time, or that do not appeal primarily to the young. I have nothing on Zen or other Sino-Japanese religions, though such groups do have growing numbers of young followers in the U.S. My access to information on such groups was limited. The same problem applied to specifically black groups like the Black Muslims, so they too were not included. Flying-saucer cults and the like have been ignored because they are too small and disorganized.

Perhaps I spent too much time on the Process (or Foundation), for they are still quite a small group. But I found them extremely interesting.

What I hope to provide in this book is a taste of the astonishing religious diversity in America today. Those who wish more than a taste can consult some of the books listed in the bibliography, or contact some of the organizations whose addresses are also provided in the back of the book.

No one can be truly objective—that is, without opinions—on a subject like this. I liked some of the groups that I covered better than others, and while I have not tried to beat anyone over the head with my own opinions, I have not tried to pretend that these opinions do not exist.

One of my own basic beliefs is that others have a right to believe whatever they wish, even if I happen to think that their beliefs are wrong, foolish or evil. So long as they are not breaking laws, like kidnapping people or performing human sacrifices, then they have a perfect right to their beliefs, and we have an obligation to try to understand them.

There is also a problem of time. A book is written at a particular time and published some months later. The reader may come upon it months or years after publication. When dealing with contemporary events, information becomes dated very quickly. Most of the religions covered in this book are quite new in America and are in a state of rapid change.

This problem was driven home to me very dramatically a short time ago. I was finishing up my section on the Process Church, and wanted to check out a few facts. The weekend before, I had visited the Process and talked with them at length. When I called the headquarters someone on the other end answered, "The Foundation." I thought I had reached the wrong number. What had happened was that there had been a major schism in the church. Up to that point the Process had been exceptionally stable. So the reader is reminded that some of the groups covered in this book may have already changed drastically or ceased to exist, and there may be new and spectacular religious stars in the sky that are not mentioned here.

But enough warnings, explanations and excuses. Ultimately a book must stand on its own.

The New Christians

The Children of God

They believe that the world is about to come to an end, and that if you don't hear their message you may be lost forever. They freely admit that they will go to practically any lengths to bring that message to your attention.

They often shock people, and they mean to. The hour is too late, they say, to stand on false dignity.

In 1974 they were going up to people on the street saying, "I am a toilet—are you?"

In the early winter of 1973 a group of them, in robes, gathered in front of the United Nations in New York City with signs warning of the arrival of the comet Kohoutek and how it was an omen that the end of the world was near.

Some years earlier a procession of them, wearing red sackcloth, ashes daubed on their faces, wooden yokes around their necks and one earring, and carrying wooden staves and signs, came to the

funeral of Senator Everett Dirksen of Illinois, proclaiming that he
had been the last public official in America to really care about the
Bible.

"They" are the Children of God, or COGs for short. Despite
their love of the theatrical, the COGs are a real honest-to-goodness,
hard-sell, fanatical Bible-believing group of thoroughly apocalyptic Christians. They see the world as we know it coming to an end
soon, probably within the next twenty years, and are preparing
themselves for the "Time of Troubles" which they believe will fore-
shadow "the End."

Because they are holy, and the rest of the world, or the System as
they prefer to call it, is thoroughly ungodly, they feel despised and
persecuted, and they glory in this.

This is the meaning of their "I am a toilet" slogan. They see
themselves as the place where the human waste products from modern society are collected and "recycled." "Out of the tank of every
toilet comes God's fresh clean water to wash away man's defile-
ment!" The sentiment of collecting the lowest of the low is hardly
new among Christians, but the slogan is an arresting one, and is
offered as both a shock and a challenge.

The COGs' theatrical and often downright bizarre behavior has
led some to assume that they are not serious. This is a mistake, for
they are very earnest.

To say that the COGs are controversial would be to describe
their position in the mildest possible terms. They have been accused
of being everything from agents of the Devil to confidence tricksters. But probably the most common charge leveled against them
is that they are hypocrites who talk of love but preach hate and
who try to pose as good Bible-believing Christians but practice
things that are abhorrent to most fundamentalists. The COGs have
been accused of getting money from people under false pretenses
and lying about their lives and goals.

Many of the charges are actually true, but to call the COGs
hypocrites is to misunderstand them, and in fact to miss the real
depth of their belief. If one has to pin a label on them, antinomian
would probably fit best. It is not a term frequently used today. The

word "antinomian" has been applied to Christian sects of the past in which members believe that because they were true Christians, the grace of God has released them from the necessity of obeying traditional political or moral laws. Thus, it is possible to lie to or cheat the people of "the World" (for the world is irredeemably evil) and yet still not be a liar or a cheat in the eyes of God. Indeed it is considered necessary to use the world's worst weapons against it to protect God's chosen but persecuted few. The COGs use the biblical phrase, "spoiling Egypt," or the modern one, "ripping off the system."

To the outsider there may seem little effective difference between this sort of antinomianism and hypocrisy, or plain lying, but the difference is extremely important to the believer. The COGs are not confidence tricksters, nor are they self-deluded fools. Dr. Will Herberg, author of the book *Protestant-Catholic-Jew*, believes that they may very well evolve into a small but permanent Protestant denomination.

The Children of God are the creation of an enigmatic fellow named David Berg, a man now in his late fifties. Berg's parents had been traveling evangelists of a fairly traditional stripe. According to COG legend, his mother, Virginia Brandt Berg, had predicted that God had great things in store for young David, but for a long time this prophecy seemed destined to remained unfulfilled. David Berg's early life was utterly undistinguished. He is said to have briefly served as a pastor to a primarily Indian congregation in Arizona, but quit because he could not make enough money to support his growing family. In the 1940s the Berg family moved to California where Berg worked as a sort of public relations man for radio evangelist Fred Jordan. But Berg and Jordan quarreled, and David Berg, his wife, four children, and some of their spouses hit the road in search of fresh territory to be conquered for Christ. They finally settled in Huntington Beach, California, where Virginia Brandt Berg was living.

Berg's big opportunity came in 1967 or 1968 when he was made director of "Teen Challenge," a Christian coffee house in Huntington Beach. Coffee houses as a means of attracting teen-agers to

Christ had become popular in many mainline church circles. But from the very beginning Berg showed that he was not going to run any ordinary ministry for the disaffected young.

Berg was not content merely to get young people off drugs, and into church and straight society in general. He wanted "one hundred percent discipleship." That meant cutting all ties with home, family, church and established society, living communally and spending all of one's time in spreading Berg's version of Christianity to other young people. Within a few months there were a dozen or so young men living in Berg's coffee house.

Today David Berg is very much a man of mystery. He lives in seclusion somewhere—most rumors place him in a small village in England. He grants no interviews to outsiders, and in fact, most of the members of the Children of God have never seen him, and would not know him if they saw him. Yet he runs the Children of God autocratically, exercising control through his wife and children and their families and a group of trusted associates from his early days. He makes his thoughts and orders known through an endless series of pamphlets and directives which he signs Moses, MO or now more commonly Moses David. Some of his writings are for the public, others for members or leaders only.

There is no evidence that David Berg possesses a particularly magnetic personality, yet he was able to inspire his early followers with an almost fanatic loyalty, and he was able to impart to them his apocalyptic vision of the world. In 1968 California was swept by "earthquake fever," a feeling that there was going to be a great earthquake and a large portion of the state was simply going to sink into the sea. This fever was fed by a number of occult groups who had all sorts of prophecies of the great earthquake, but it also infected many Christian fundamentalists, for whom catastrophic events heralding Judgment Day seem always at hand. California was viewed as a new Sodom that should be destroyed for its wickedness anyway. One of those most severely afflicted with earthquake fever was David Berg.

Berg, in his new role as Moses, gathered his family and followers, numbering about fifty at that time, into a couple of converted school buses, and led them out of the doomed land. The failure of the prophecy did not unduly upset Berg or his followers. They were launched on a new career.

For about eight months Berg and his followers led an uncertain existence, drifting through the southwest, sleeping in the buses and depending on charity for food. Often they said they were reduced to eating grass, and COGs now compare this period of wandering with the time that the Children of Israel spent wandering in the wilderness.

It was about this time that Berg's little tribe acquired the name Children of God. The group was first called Teens for Christ, and briefly, Revolutionaries for Jesus. Their slogan is still "Revolution for Jesus." No one seems to know exactly where the name Children of God came from, but a COG leader told me it had first been applied to them by a newspaper reporter.

During this period the Children of God first began to come to public notice. A scruffy-looking crew of COGs, bearded and often barefoot, would march into a church while the service was in progress and sit down in the front pews or on the floor. They stood out in stark contrast to the clean, well-fed and often self-satisfied members of the regular congregation. Usually they were thrown out, but such an incident made good newspaper copy and Berg's flock may have tripled in size during the period of wandering.

In early 1970 Berg's old employer, Fred Jordan, rescued the Children from their wandering and allowed them to settle on a desolate 400-acre ranch (dubbed the "Texas Soul Clinic") about seventy miles west of Fort Worth. He also allowed them to take over a nearly defunct skid row rescue mission in Los Angeles.

Fred Jordan is a fairly traditional fundamentalist evangelist, with the usual right-wing political leanings. Why then did he give shelter to this far from traditional communal group, led by a man whom he had once fired? Jordan claims that the COGs tricked him by hiding their real aims, and this is certainly possible. But there may be another reason. Like most traditional evangelists, Jordan was having no successs at all in reaching the long-haired youth of the counterculture that had grown up in the 1960s. These

hippies terrified his conservative traditional followers. By presenting the highly visible COGs on his television show he could look
like he was reaching those kids.

The appeal worked for a while. The COGs were presented as a
bunch of long-haired ex-junkies who had been converted to Christ
and 100 per cent Americanism. This was a complete perversion
of COG doctrine, and in fact they had no respect at all for
Jordan's brand of Christianity. Just who was fooling whom is hard
to say, but the COGs did prove to be potent fund raisers.

This marriage of convenience was doomed from the start. When
Jordan moved from merely misrepresenting COG doctrine to actually trying to interfere with the running of the group, the break
came. There was a nasty dispute over who owned property purchased with funds raised by the COGs. Jordan tried to get one of
the stubborn COG leaders replaced, but he failed and the group
moved out of all of the Jordan-owned properties. Jordan had tried
to persuade some of them to stay in the relative comfort he had
provided for them, but not one was swayed.

The COGs left behind thousands of dollars' worth of improvements that they had made on the properties, as well as some of their
own personal belongings. But during their stay they had gained
nearly a thousand new converts, and they felt that they had gotten
the better part of the bargain.

The COGs dispersed to colonies (they dislike the term communes) throughout the country, and apparently decided that they
never were going to be tied down to property again. They will rent
space for their colonies, or they will settle in an area if invited to
do so, but as a matter of policy they don't buy property and are always ready to be on the move. Berg has written, ". . . moving is one
of our professions! We're Gospel Gypsies, having no certain resting
place! This world is not our home. . . ."

From their colonies, COG members go out into the area, particularly to places where young people may gather, in an attempt to
make converts.

Ronald M. Enroth, Edward E. Ericson, Jr., and C. Breckinridge Peters, authors of *The Jesus People,* offer this description of

a group of COGs "witnessing"—that is, trying to make converts on the street.

> In one case, we observed a young man chasing another down the sidewalk, waving a Bible in one hand, and shouting, "Don't run from the Spirit brother!" On another occasion we confronted a girl who was obviously a babe in Christ [a new COG member] and her male companion. He said that he had been a Catholic and a transvestite; just one year earlier he had walked on that very same street wearing women's clothes. He explained that the Spirit had taken away all of this upon his conversion. The girl asked us if we were saved. When we said yes, she took up her guitar and sang for us. We asked her if the Children of God spoke in tongues. She gave us an impromptu demonstration right on Hollywood Boulevard.

Usually COG colonies are not particularly popular, either with their neighbors or local officials, and they are often pressured to move. In the early 1970s there may have been some sixty COG colonies scattered throughout the U.S. The largest probably contained about seventy residents, but colony membership was never stable, as individuals were shifted frequently from one colony to another. New colonies were constantly opening as old ones closed.

The high water mark of COG membership in the United States was reached around early 1972 when the group had some three thousand members in colonies from coast to coast. Since that time the number of members in America has declined, though worldwide the membership has at least remained stable, and perhaps has risen. The reason for the decline in the U.S. is that Moses David is now leading his flock out of America, as he once led them out of California. He is convinced that America is going to be destroyed, and soon.

Berg himself seems to have left America in late 1970 or early 1971. COG missionaries followed him and set up colonies in vari-

ous parts of Europe and Mexico. Many of their overseas converts
came from among the crowd of young American expatriates and
were really not very different from the converts they had made in
the States.

When I interviewed members of the Children of God in late
1972, most of them were either on their way to Europe and Latin
America or planning to go there in the near future. When asked
why they were leaving America they gave variety of reasons. First
they said that there were uncounted millions in the world who
needed Jesus. After further conversation they indicated that America had largely become barren territory as far as conversions were
concerned, and that they were facing great persecution and hostility. This they interpreted as a sign of the approaching Time of
Troubles and the inevitable destruction of America. This destruction was probably going to come about as the result of some sort of
bloody revolution, though they were not specific. The fall of America would be yet another sign of the final end.

The Children of God see themselves as forming the basis of a
nation. They believe that under God's special protection they will
survive the coming Armageddon and become the foundation on
which the millennial world to follow the destruction will be based.
They are to be the founders of a New Jerusalem on this earth.

For a time it appeared that the COGs actually believed they
would be allowed to settle in Israel, thus fulfilling biblical prophecy
about returning to the Holy Land. But Israel has never welcomed
proselytizing Christian sects, and they received no encouragement.
More recently the COGs have turned their eyes to other parts of
the Middle East, notably Libya, which is really in North Africa
but was at least part of the biblical world.

Why Libya? Because the Children of God have developed a relationship with Colonel Mu'ammar Gaddafi (also spelled Muammar el-Qaddafi), Libya's youthful revolutionary leader. Gaddafi is
himself an oddity in world politics. He is both anti-Communist and
anticapitalist, as are the Children of God. He is leader of a large
underdeveloped country, but one with immensely rich oil reserves.
He is ascetic, mystical and fanatically religious, but there is or
should be a problem as far as the Children of God are concerned,
for Gaddafi is a fanatically religious Moslem.

Dramatic public demonstrations like this one in Los Angeles have often been used by the Children of God to gain publicity.

And yet David Berg has hailed Gaddafi as something just short of a new Messiah. In a 1973 pamphlet entitled *Gaddaffi's Third World* Berg wrote:

> May the Godly youth of the world unite against both Christless capitalism, *and* Godless communism, and create a *New* World free of *both* where *all* are free under God himself!—Amen! Hallelujah!
>
> May Allah bless us who do His works! And may God bless and keep His brave young prophet Mu'ammar Gaddafi, who speaks his words to save the world, and all who follow him!—In Jesus' name, Amen!

Gaddafi, who rarely even sees westerners, entertained two of Berg's children in his tent, and he wrote a song for them. It is hard to imagine how even the most generous kind of biblical interpretation would allow the Children of God to follow a Moslem. One might speculate that they regard Gaddafi as a latter-day Fred Jordan, a powerful figure with whom they are willing to compromise in order to obtain certain advantages. What Gaddafi sees in the Children of God is anybody's guess. In any event, by mid-1974 Gaddafi was himself in serious trouble in the Arab world, and even in his own country. The amount that he would or could do for the COGs in the future is highly uncertain.

The Children of God's flirtation with one of the most virulent of the anti-Israeli Arab leaders brings up the frequently repeated charge that the COGs are anti-Semitic. And in fact, a few of David Berg's pamphlets do sound like throwbacks to the anti-Semitic propaganda of pre–World War II days. One of the early Nazi charges was that "Jewish banking interests" were somehow manipulating the world money market, causing inflation and ruining good Christians. In 1974, David Berg, in a pamphlet on inflation, wrote:

> *THEN IT CAME TO ME* as plain as anything: "Well *what* do you think is *doing* it? *Why* is the Dollar inflating?"—This is what's doing it: The Jews are selling out their European currencies and buying Dollars instead! The Jewish banking interests apparently are buying Dollars and Pounds and European money deliberately to try to hurt England and Europe for the stand they took on the Mideast! So they're dumping their European currencies and buying Dollars to favour their friend America and punish Europe!

On the other hand, Berg has claimed that he is Jewish, and a fair number of COG converts are Jewish. He has often written equally angry diatribes against Christians.

Berg's obsession with political developments in the Middle East is traditional among apocalyptic-minded fundamentalists. They believe that the battle of Armageddon—that final battle between the forces of Satan and the forces of Christ—will be fought in the ancient Holy Land, at a spot that is now part of modern Israel. Each political development in that turbulent part of the world is looked upon as yet another fulfillment of biblical prophecy, and another sign that the end is near.

In the late 1973 Berg issued a pamphlet with the title *Israel Invaded!* The subtitle read, "Armageddon on the way! It won't be long *now*! Are you ready?" The pamphlet, issued shortly after the outbreak of the October war between Israel and the Arabs, predicted not only the destruction of Israel, but the destruction of America and probably the whole world. As the war ground down to a cease-fire, if not a permanent peace, the COGs were still predicting that the end would come soon. They had just been a bit premature in interpreting the signs.

The Children of God do not look only to the Middle East for signs of the coming end. There are also signs in the sky. In 1973 there was great excitement about the approach of the comet Kohoutek. The comet was to pass in the vicinity of the earth around Christmas time and many astronomers predicted that it would be the brightest comet of the century. (In fact there have not been any really bright comets for over a century.) There were even predictions that the comet would be six times as bright as the moon. For centuries people have considered comets to be potent omens of something awful. The scientific predictions excited a lot of other speculation. One of those who seized upon Kohoutek avidly was David Berg. He dubbed the comet the Christmas Monster, and members of the Children of God, dressed in homespun robes and carrying long wooden staves, stood in front of the United Nations building in New York City with signs warning of the approaching end. In one of Berg's many writings on the subject of Kohoutek he said, "*You* in the *U.S.* have only until *January* [1974] to get *out* of the States before some kind of disaster, destruction or judgment of God is to fall because of America's wickedness. . . . *Now* is the *time*! It's *later* than you *think*! *Hallelujah*! The *End* is near!"

As it turned out, Kohoutek was a complete fizzle for everyone but professional astronomers. Far from being six times as bright as the moon, it was virtually invisible to the naked eye. The time of the comet's closest approach to earth passed with no more than the usual disasters. But the Children of God were undismayed. There were plenty of other signs of the coming end.

The tone and even the appearance of David Berg's writings would be familiar to anyone who has ever worked in a newspaper or magazine office. Editors get a regular stream of letters and privately printed publications from people who believe that they are being persecuted because they are God's chosen, or have discovered some great truth the rest of the world has failed to recognize. These letters, like Berg's, are filled with capitalizations, strange made-up words, underlined words, dashes and loads of explanation points. They are often written in colored ink, just as Berg's pamphlets are often printed in colored ink, which makes them hard to read. As soon as a heavily underlined letter written in colored ink reaches a busy editor's desk, he is likely to toss it in the wastebasket as a piece of crank mail. But to dismiss David Berg as a crank would be a serious mistake. Strange as his ideas may sound to us, he has attracted a following of thousands of devoted, and often very talented, young people.

In the early 1970s it was easy to miss the genuinely radical side of the Children of God, particularly when they took pains to hide it. A glowing article in the *El Paso Herald Post* of November 1971 describes a visit to a COG colony in these terms: "Their faces have a wholesome, scrubbed look; their hair is neatly combed, their clothing spotless. Their happy smiles, courtesy, and gentleness and kindness to each other set them apart." The article was illustrated with pictures of a half dozen or so clean, smiling COGs. During this period they went in for short hair and clean shaves.

When NBC News did a special on the Jesus movement in January 1971 they treated the COGs as just another Jesus group, a little more devoted than the rest but not essentially different. The coverage gained the COGs many new members.

But about that time ominous rumors began to spread about the Children of God. Parents of members began to complain that their children had been "kidnapped," "brainwashed" and "taught to hate." There were stories of COG members being kept in virtual slavery. A group of parents of members and ex-members met in San Diego to form a national Parents Committee of Free Our Children from the Children of God (FREECOG). FREECOG held demonstrations, and denounced the Children of God in the strongest possible terms. Ex-members got up to tell how they had "escaped the clutches" of the COGs, and they often described the group as "subversive" or even "satanic." In fact, the ex-members, confessing how they had been "saved from the Children of God," sounded very much like the members of the Children of God confessing how they had been saved from the sins of the world.

Someone flilched a packet of David Berg's correspondence, meant only for members, and published it. Up to that time Berg's more exotic ideas were not public knowledge. These letters implied that sexual practice within COG colonies was far from traditional. NBC News went back for another look, and produced a devastatingly critical hour-long documentary. COG leaders were evasive in answering reporters' questions, particularly about Berg.

The COGs' number one nemesis was also beginning to emerge. He is Ted Patrick, a former minor official in the state government of California. Patrick has made his reputation "saving" young people from groups like the Children of God. "Saving" an individual has often involved physically removing him, and then holding him against his will for "deprogramming." Patrick's deprogramming appears to be something halfway between psychological pressure and exorcism. Though Patrick usually works with the cooperation of parents, some of those he has attempted to save are of legal age, and so his efforts look suspiciously like kidnapping. Most of the time, local law enforcement officials, who don't like the Children of God anyway, turn a blind eye to his activities. Some of the subjects of Patrick's deprogramming have expressed gratitude to him. Others have escaped back to the groups they were taken from, and a few have taken Patrick to court. In mid-1974 he was convicted in Denver, Colorado, in connection with deprogramming members from another fundamentalist group. How this conviction will affect future deprogramming is unknown.

A number of serious charges have been leveled against the Children of God by parents of members, disillusioned ex-members and occasionally by law enforcement officials. One of the most serious involves the way in which the Children of God get their money.

The COGs whom I observed, and my impressions seem fairly typical, lived in modest though not harsh circumstances. Nobody was eating grass anymore, but there was no steak on the table either. Cheap fare like hot dogs, potatoes and pasta made up the bulk of the diet. Still, running the COGs has to be a fairly expensive operation, and yet nobody works. When I asked where they got their money, the usual answer I got was "God provides." They also said that they had members who served as "procurers" or "provisioners" who went around to local stores getting dented cans and day-old bread. But clearly there have to be other sources of income and probably the most significant of these is the members themselves. When someone joins up with the COGs he or she must sign over everything he owns. "Some churches tithe their membership," one COG elder told me frankly. "We take it all at once." In one of his private letters to COG leadership Berg said: "This is where the money comes from—NEW DISCIPLES! This is why it is impossible for us to stop growing. We have to grow to stay financially stable." There are, of course, several biblical references to forsaking all wealth to follow God, and the COGs quote these freely. COGs have been accused of deliberately cultivating wealthier members, but even a poor individual, if he owns a car and has a small bank account, may be able to add several thousands to the COG treasury upon joining.

In addition, COGs have been accused of having members put heavy pressure on their parents to continue contributions. The COGs also receive an unknown amount in donations from individuals who like the group. Financial records for the organization have been impossible to obtain, but there is no evidence that the Children of God are a money-making racket. Most of the money the COGs collect appears to be used in the day-to-day operations of the group.

The scariest charge made against the COGs is that they "brainwash" their members. Horrified parents have testified that their COG children appeared "drugged," "glassy-eyed," "in a trance" or in a "hypnotic state," and that they quoted Bible verses in a parrot-like fashion.

The problem with such a charge is that no one is really sure what brainwashing means, or if it means anything at all. One of the first to apply the term brainwashing to the COGs was Fred Jordan,

at the time he was still friendly with them. "Sure we brainwash 'em," he said. "We clean their brains." To most people, however, brainwashing has a far more sinister connotation. It implies prison camp conditions and some sort of drastic mental conditioning.

The testimony of ex-COGs reinforces the brainwashing charge. They said that after they joined they were never left alone. For months they were forced to read and memorize selected biblical passages and attend long and fatiguing "Bible study" sessions. In some colonies there were even supposed to be loud-speakers that broadcast Bible quotes into every room. They also said that the colonies were well-guarded, and that they had to feign illness or use other forms of trickery to escape.

My own observations do not support the most extreme of these charges. The COG colony I visited, while hardly a model of democracy, was not a prison camp either. There were no fences or guards, and though the elders kept a pretty close eye on everyone who came and went, "escape" would have been relatively easy. The new members, or babes, didn't know their Bible very well, and did tend to give very standard and mechanical responses to questions. But no more mechanical, I think, than a schoolchild repeating a recently learned lesson.

The secret to the COGs' control over their members, and they certainly do exercise control, is not so much what happens after a new member gets into a colony, but what has happened to him before. Many of the COGs whom I met told of being at the absolute bottom physically, emotionally and spiritually at the time they joined. Typically, they had broken with their parents long before meeting the COGs, had spent some months or even years wandering about and had often been heavy drug users. To such individuals the total control and absolute certainty of life in the COGs was a relief, a positive joy. They were fed and clothed, they had no decisions to make, they never had to be alone and they had come to believe that what they were doing was absolutely right. The resentments that many of them already felt toward their parents, and society in general, were incorporated into a cosmic theology.

Many parents have charged that COGs are taught to hate their parents. The COGs deny this charge, though not very strongly,

and they continually cite Jesus' statement, "And a man's foes shall
be they of his own household." It is quite natural and understand-
able for distraught parents to blame the COGs for alienating their
children, but in truth many of these children were lost to their
parents anyway.

Others have charged that the COGs had promised draft exemp-
tion to male members, and have provided hiding places for members on the run from the law or their parents. Members are constantly shifted from colony to colony.

All COGs adopt biblical names upon joining, and this makes
them hard to trace. The police may be looking for John Jones, but
the COGs could quite honestly say they don't know any John
Jones, for he is known to everybody as Jethro. The COGs formally
deny that they hide anybody from the law, but David Berg's
private instructions to leaders tell a different story:

> You must not interfere with an officer who comes with
> a mental warrant—or you're in legal trouble! You can
> ask to see the warrant—make sure who it's for, and while
> you are stalling, someone else can inform the disciple in-
> volved, who then has a perfect right to run out the back
> door if he wants to.

Most of the COGs' security appears to be aimed at heading off
parents trying to recapture their children, rather than keeping
members themselves from running away.

COGs get their converts from a variety of religious backgrounds.
The bulk of the members—hippies, former drug users, ex-pros-
titutes and so forth—usually come from homes in which religion
was not particularly important. There is a high proportion of ex-
Catholics and Jews in the COGs. But there is a second important
though smaller class of members. These are individuals who came
from strongly fundamentalist backgrounds, and already believed
in the literal truth of the Bible before joining the COGs. They
joined because they felt their own churches were not fundamentalist
enough, or had somehow "sold out." They wanted a more rigid

Children of God have a rather grim reputation, but joyful singing and dancing is part of daily life at the COG colonies.

and radical form of Christianity. While these members may have flirted with other Jesus groups, they rarely went through the experiences with dope, sex and wandering common among the bulk of COGs. It is from these fundamentalist youth that the COG leadership is drawn. Their dedication, energy and skill is impressive. While David Berg and his family control the Children of God as a whole, these second-line leaders, or elders, exercise absolute control within the individual colonies.

At first glance it is a little difficult to tell that a COG colony has any leaders at all. Everyone looks the same, and no one has an official title. But it doesn't take long to notice that there are always a few individuals who step forward to greet visitors. The same people always answer the phone, and when a babe gets asked an uncomfortable question, he always looks toward one of the elders for help. Wherever a visitor goes there always seems to be one of the elders around. The elders are also the ones who have read the Bible and not merely memorized selected passages. It isn't easy to confound them with a biblical question.

There is a good deal of mystery about the COGs' sexual practices. Those I talked to said that strict monogamy was the rule within COG colonies. But when pressed on exactly how this worked, they became vague. In fact, it is quite well established that marriages within COG colonies are arranged by the elders. The women, at least, have no choice over whom they will "marry," and all marriages are performed by COG elders and not registered legally. In general women in COG communities hold extremely inferior roles, and perhaps because of this there seem to be far fewer women than men in the COGs.

Arranged "marriages" may not be the whole story either, for there have also been charges that upper-level COG leaders are allowed numerous sexual partners, just like the Hebrew patriarchs. It isn't hard to justify polygamy with the Bible. In fact, even in his public writings David Berg comes pretty close to endorsing it.

Many of the Jesus groups look upon sex as a necessary evil, a means of reproduction rather than a positive enjoyment. This clearly is not the attitude of the Children of God, but they are also very interested in procreation. Berg has written, "Be fruitful and multiply—that's one of the first principles of this outfit in more ways than one. We believe in multiplication—that's part of the game—in more ways than one!"

Most of the women in the colony that I visited were either pregnant or caring for infants. They were opposed to abortion, birth control and having children in hospitals. Children are born in the colony, without the aid of doctors. All the other members stand around singing and praying during delivery. I was told that there were rarely any complications in deliveries. One of the COG publications provided readers with a comic strip explaining how to deliver a baby.

What are all of these children for? Remember that the COGs

view themselves as God's own nation, the small band of survivors of the coming apocalypse. They, along with their children, will inhabit the New World. Since the destruction is only about twenty years away, they feel they must hurry.

Before I visited the COGs I had already heard most of the criticisms and rumors. I was rather apprehensive, expecting to find a group of grim fanatics. Their philosophy may be grim, and their practices fanatical to outsiders, but the COGs themselves, from the elders to the babes, appeared dedicated and happy—they were not the hollow-eyed, brainwashed robots that are described so often. The Bible classes that I attended were long, repetitious and dull to me. and I practically fell asleep. But the COGs enjoyed them. And their celebrations were genuinely joyful. They have their own gospel songs, usually sung to electrically amplified accompaniment. They dance a sort of modified hora, not well but with great enthusiasm. And they are always shouting "Thank you, Jesus" with feeling. They give vent to a full range of human emotion, from love of Jesus to hatred of "the system."

On my first visit to the COGs I met a young man who had wandered into the colony just a few hours earlier. He had apparently just come down off a drug high. He was nearly incoherent, physically shaky and he cried a lot. He babbled out a story the essence of which was that he didn't think anybody liked him. He was a fat, ugly kid from a poor family and not terribly bright. Life had not been kind to him and he didn't think he stood a chance in the world.

I saw him again a few weeks later, after he had undergone what some have called the sinister COG "brainwashing." He looked a lot better. He could talk coherently. Sure, a lot of it was undigested Bible quotes, but between the quotes he was able to carry on a conversation. He was, at least for the time being, happy. There were people who cared for him, and cared about him.

In the colony David Berg is a remote figure. Even the Bible reading may well be a secondary activity for most of the members. I got the feeling that it wasn't brainwashing, hypnotism or fences that held the COGs. It wasn't even obedience to God's word, or the desire to survive the coming apocalypse. The binding force, I believe, is a strong sense of community and exclusivity. The feeling of being a little band of brothers and sisters, despised by, but better than, the rest of the world.

The Jesus People

Sometimes it is rather difficult to decide whether something called the Jesus movement ever really existed or if it was just a creation of the media. Terms like Jesus People, Jesus Freaks, Street Christians and the like have been tossed about freely since the late 1960s. They have been used to describe everything from the Children of God to youthful followers of Billy Graham.

It sounds as though millions of young people have become involved in a new and intensely spirited form of Christianity. But the image is misleading. The thousands upon thousands of young people who attended the Billy Graham–dominated Explo '72 in the Cotton Bowl in Dallas can not properly be called Jesus People. While they listened to rock bands and sermons about Jesus, and the whole event was called a "religious Woodstock," it was in reality just a big gathering of rather conventional young Christians from fundamentalist backgrounds. They were not dropouts converted to Christ, they were sons and daughters of good church people who had never left home.

It has long been a practice of evangelists like Billy Graham to tailor the appearance of their events to catch the public attention or be in line with current fashions. But the message remains the same. Events like the highly publicized Explo '72 are nothing more than standard establishment evangelism, with electric guitars and a soft rock beat substituted for the traditional cabinet organ and sentimental hymns.

Productions like *Jesus Christ Superstar* and *Godspell,* bumper stickers which read "Honk if you love Jesus," and genuinely grotesque items like Jesus Christ jockey shorts and Jesus Christ bikinis are all part of the marketing system and pop culture rather than religion or any desire for a spiritual rebirth.

The Children of God, as we have seen, are not commercial and they are certainly not establishment Christians. If a Jesus movement exists they are part of it, quite a large part. But they are on the fringe and very much alone. While the COGs have pulled in influential converts from other Jesus groups, those who have not converted hate them. Most other Jesus People think of the COGs as fanatics at best.

What's left? Somewhere between Billy Graham and David Berg there is a collection of churches, communes, centers, groups and newspapers that deserve the title Jesus movement, but the movement is in no sense unified. It is possible to trace the origins and history of the Jesus movement in only the most general sort of way.

Most observers agree that the movement began in California in the late 1960s. Areas like San Francisco's Haight-Ashbury, or Los Angeles' Sunset Strip, were magnets for runaways, dropouts from a straight society, drug users—in short, for that mass of young people who were labeled hippies. The hippies were a highly visible, highly publicized and highly vocal downtrodden minority. Unlike other downtrodden minorities, however, the hippies often came from solid middle-class homes. Society was more interested in them than in the genuinely poor.

In the past Christian missionaries had gone out to "save" the natives of Africa and Asia and the drunks on skid row. The "natives" no longer welcome or even tolerate missionaries, and social service agencies have largely taken over the drunks. So a new generation of missionaries turned to the hippies. The hippies held a triple appeal for the evangelists. First, being immersed in drugs and sex, they were the worst sort of sinners, and thus their conversion was all the more spectacular. Second, most of the hippies had to a degree rejected materialism and were looking for some sort of spiritual values. In their search they had tried drugs, occultism and a variety of exotic Eastern religions. Now, thought the new missionaries, they were ready for Christianity. Third, missionaries to the hippies got a lot of publicity.

Ronald M. Enroth, Edward E. Ericson, Jr., and C. Breckinridge Peters, authors of *The Jesus People,* one of the most complete and reliable books on the movement, wrote:

> There are several ministries that began independently in 1967 and 1968 which lie behind the Jesus Movement of today. Lonnie Frisbee, a leading Jesus Freak, has a fascinating explanation for the rise and success of such ministries at that period. He suggests that the Six-Day War of June 1967 between Israel and the surrounding Arab nations set the stage for the last days before Christ's second coming. When Israel regained her long-lost territory, a prophecy was fulfilled that signaled the beginning of the end times.

Perhaps the fulfillment of biblical prophecy wasn't the reason the Jesus movement got started, but it gives you a good idea of the type of Christianity that became popular. The Jesus People were biblical literalists, or fundamentalists, and deeply apocalyptic. They preached an emotional rather than an intellectual brand of Christianity. Indeed, the entire movement has a decidedly anti-intellectual cast.

To many conventional Christians the rise of the Jesus movement looked like a hopeful sign. Here was a generation that had appeared lost in sin, adopting old-fashioned traditional Christian values. Instead of turning on with drugs, they were "turning on with Jesus." Some saw the Jesus People as the leading edge of a "new spiritual awakening" that evangelists had been predicting for years. Billy Graham announced, "Millions are rejecting the materialism, the secularism, the skepticism of their elders. They are on a gigantic search for reality, purpose, and meaning. I seriously doubt if there has ever been a time in history when so many young people are professing conversion to Christ at this very hour."

Peter Michelmore begins his book *Back to Jesus* with this enthusiastic phrase: "The Holy Spirit is abroad in the land. He came like a thief in the night, around the turn and into the decade of the sixties, touching a life here and there, then seeming to wait offstage for the call to lead the greatest spiritual renaissance in the history of the United States."

To many sincere Christians, in and out of the Jesus movement, it looked as though the much talked about "Age of Aquarius" was really going to be an "Age of Jesus."

But there were doubters. Many people within the various Christian denominations warned that the movement was shallow, and would soon disappear just like any other fad. Sour grapes from the establishment, retorted the enthusiasts.

But by the early 1970s it had become obvious that the doubts were well-founded, and that the size and influence of the Jesus movement had been greatly exaggerated. Typical was the fate of Arthur Blessitt, the "Minister of Sunset Strip." Blessitt had attracted enormous publicity with his mission on the Strip. But by the early seventies Blessitt's Strip mission was dead, and his attempt to convert the Times Square area of New York was not very successful. The thousands upon thousands of converts he had claimed have melted away.

Other leaders of the Jesus movement have become discouraged when their flocks, instead of growing, began to shrink until they were reduced to a mere handful. At least part of the appeal of the Jesus movement was the promise that it would sweep the world quickly. When it failed to do that, many Jesus People were puzzled and disappointed.

Of course, even a temporary involvement with the Jesus movement may have a permanent effect upon an individual, but many observers of the movement fear that the effect will not necessarily be a good one. The authors of *The Jesus People* comment, "Just as there is no anti-Communist like an ex-Communist, so there is no anti-Christian like an ex-Jesus person. Such is the way with true believers . . . who have lost the faith."

Many early Jesus People professed an intense hatred of organization of any kind, contending that the Holy Spirit, and the Holy Spirit alone, would carry them forward, without any need for supporting institutions. Yet those Jesus People who have remained with the movement are generally those who have been attached to tightly structured groups, often under the sway of a compelling leader or leaders.

By most accounts the Children of God is the largest of such organizations—and its total membership, a mere 3,000, will give you some idea of just how exaggerated the size of the Jesus movement was. But the COGs are not the only survivors.

Another group, nearly as controversial as the COGs, is the Christian Foundation, the creation of Tony and Susan Alamo. One is tempted to say it is a creation of Hollywood, for its founders are both very much show biz.

Tony Alamo, formerly Bernard Hoffman, was born in Montana of Jewish parents. He changed his name when he went into show business "because Italians at the time were making it big as singers." But he soon passed from the role of performer to that of promoter. He claims to have been an extremely successful impresario of pop and rock musicians, numbering among his clients such big names as Sonny and Cher. He even had his own recording label, "Talamo." "I had the Twenty Original Hits, twenty smash hits on one album, Oldies but Goodies for $2.98. I made loads of money. I was making more money than General Motors," he has said.

Then in 1964, at the height of his success, Tony Alamo thought he heard the voice of God threatening to kill him unless he gave up the life he was living and went out to preach the gospel. It was a very unsettling experience, but Tony did not immediately abandon show business.

The real change in his life came later, after he met and married Susan Fleetwood, a former small-time movie actress. Susan too had been reared in a Jewish home, but had converted to Christianity quite early in life, and had given up acting for evangelism.

Together the Alamos prowled the streets of Hollywood passing out fundamentalist tracts and talking to all who stopped to listen. Soon they attracted a following which would crowd into their rented house each night to hear Susie and Tony preach. With financial help from a Christian businessman's group they moved to a larger house and continued their efforts.

Many of those attracted were addicts, and the Alamos' following was (and still is) made up largely of former addicts "cured" of their addiction through the Alamos' efforts. But neither the neighbors nor the police appreciated the presence of the crowd of ex-addicts and other strange-looking people which gathered nightly at the Alamo house, and so, again with financial help from the Christian businessmen, they moved to a converted restaurant on the outskirts of Saugus, California, about fifty miles or an hour and a half drive from Hollywood.

At the Alamos' Christian Foundation, full-time followers live communally, though the Alamos reject the use of the word "commune" because it implies drugs, free sex and a lot of other things that are very definitely not part of the Christian Foundation.

Men and women not only live in separate houses, the houses are quite a distance from one another. Even something as innocent as hand holding is strictly forbidden, and conversation between the sexes is allowed only at mealtimes. Marriage is permitted if approved by the Alamos. But before the wedding the couple must endure a separation of about ninety days for prayer and fasting. The ratio of men to women in the group is about three to one.

Naturally drugs, drinking and social dancing are prohibited, but oddly, smoking is not. Some critics feel that this is only because Tony himself has never been able to drop the habit. The Alamos admit that smoking is a sin, but only a "sin of the flesh," not a "sin of the soul."

Control of the group is exercised by the Alamos through a

network of trusted elders or overseers. Nobody works outside of the foundation, and it is supported entirely by donations. Since the Alamos' brand of Christianity is more standard than that of the COGs, they get more help from outside Christian organizations.

Several times a week young "witness teams" from the Alamos' foundation make the drive to Hollywood, passing out tracts warning the reader "Repent of your Sins! Jesus is Coming Soon" and inviting them to come to one of the regularly scheduled meetings at the foundation. There is a free daily shuttle bus service for the curious.

There are a number of oddities about the Alamos' Christian Foundation that observers have found both curious and unnerving. Many of the Jesus groups stress God's love, and even the Children of God are continually telling visitors how "Jesus Loves You." The Alamos' converts are uncompromisingly grim; their message is a harsh "repent or be damned!" They stress God's punishment, not God's love. Says Tony of the Jesus People, "I don't like what they're preaching. They're preaching God is love. It's not true, and it's throwing a lot of people into the pits of hell." The Alamos,

Mass public baptisms like this one in the Brandywine Creek near Wilmington, Delaware, have been staged by Jesus People.

however, do not reject the name Jesus People entirely—they even claim to have started the movement.

The Alamos' Christian Foundation does not go in for big crosses, fish symbols, Jesus buttons or the weird outfits often affected by the Children of God. The members dress plainly, even shabbily, and many observers feel that they look downright undernourished.

The appearance of the disciples of the Alamos is in marked contrast to their own. Both Tony and Susie dress well and Tony is often described as a flashy dresser. Susie, who was compared with Lana Turner in her acting days, still tries to keep up the old image. The pair also live well when compared with the austere conditions that prevail at the foundation. They drive around in a large comfortable car while the foundation members make do with broken-down old vans and trucks. These obvious inequities have made the Alamos the subject of a great deal of criticism and ridicule. But their followers don't seem to mind, and the Alamos are certainly not the first religious leaders in the world to have lived in material comfort while their followers groveled in miserable poverty.

Many of the other Jesus People have favored some of the newer, more modern-sounding translations of the Bible. The Alamos will have none of this. To them the King James Version is the inspired word of God and anything not in strict accordance with the King James Version is out. Indeed, the Alamos believe that the proliferation of modern translations is another sign of the coming end. The Alamos do not write their own hymns, they rely on tried and true evangelistic hymns like "When the Roll is Called Up Yonder."

Services at the Christian Foundation are rousing in an old-fashioned, foot-stomping, hand-clapping sort of way. Hymns are sung to the accompaniment of about thirty musical instruments, and at a volume that is almost painful. The Alamos' sermons are all hellfire and damnation. Says Tony:

> I know that God was not just a God of love because he threatened to kill me, and I saw these God-is-love people, little cats running around with their phony little

messages, not messages from the Bible, and I heard that
God drowned the whole world and that didn't figure out
to me. And that he barbecued Sodom and Gomorrah
and that he was gonna come back and fry everyone else
that didn't get right. So I figured, who's kidding who?

Like many others of an apocalyptic turn of mind, the Alamos
see the return of Christ within twenty years, and they expect
worldwide disasters and persecution of true Christians (mostly
themselves and their followers) to begin at almost any moment.
They are planning to move to a more remote spot as soon as
possible.

While the Alamos shun the name commune as a description for
their foundation, there are others among the Jesus People who
do not shy away from the term, and the development of Jesus
communes was one of the more notable features of the movement.
Just how many of these communes exist is difficult to say, for
most do not seek publicity, and in fact work hard at remaining as
inconspicuous as possible.

While many of the Jesus communes, like other communes,
have been short-lived, a few appear to have sunk deeper roots and
may be part of the American scene for a long time to come. One
of these was studied in detail by sociologists Mary White Harder,
James T. Richardson and Robert B. Simmonds. The sociologists
did not want to reveal the name or location of this particular
commune, so they called it Christ Commune, "a pseudonym for
one branch of what is probably the best-organized, most rapidly
growing sect in the so-called Jesus Movement. It appears to us
the group is more viable than even the much-publicized Children
of God Sect." Christ Commune is located in a western state.

At the end of 1972 the sociologists observed:

> The organization that runs Christ Commune has been in
> existence four years; it operates, in addition to the com-
> mune branch we studied, other agricultural activities, a
> small fishing fleet, and about 35 other houses across the
> country. We estimate that the sect has between 600 and

800 members overall, and financial assets of about a million dollars.

During much of the year the members of this sect live in the group's various houses that are strung out along the West Coast. There they are trained for evangelical work. But during the summer many of them gather at Christ Commune for a few months of hard agricultural labor. Work begins at 4:30 in the morning, and members do not usually go to bed until eleven.

Christ Commune had been highly successful at rehabilitating former drug users, and its success had been recognized by the courts, which occasionally remand juvenile delinquents to its custody.

Members of the Christ Commune agreed to take a battery of standard personality tests for the investigators. Their scores were compared to scores of college students. The basic finding was that the commune members were a good deal less aggressive, but also less self-confident than the college students. They were far readier to submit to counseling and the leadership of others than were the students.

At least part of the difference in scores may have been due to the commune's fundamentalist ideology, wherein man is viewed as sinful and degraded. They may well have evaluated themselves the way that they thought they were supposed to. One girl, while answering the question of whether she had self-confidence, said, "I am confident in the Lord, but I am not confident in myself. Therefore I do not have self-confidence."

A lot of people have criticized the Jesus communes and communes in general for producing people who are passive and sheep-like, but the investigators of the Christ Commune comment, "We suggest that the Christ Commune might have developed a viable life-style that differs remarkably from what our culture expects. Perhaps we should congratulate them for developing a way of life that encourages cooperation and self-abasement instead of competition and dominance."

Certainly the most self-abased group at the Christ Commune was the women, for according to the group's strict fundamentalist theology everybody is equal before the Lord, but everybody also has his "place," and the woman's place is distinctly subservient to the man's. Women did all the cooking and cleaning, and while the men also did a lot of hard work, they had some say in the decision-making process. The women had none.

Marriages within the group were encouraged (though all had to be approved by the group's leaders), but premarital sex was strictly forbidden—and this created real problems. The group's theology held that a woman's body is a temptation to sin; therefore women in the commune found it necessary to dress as unattractively as possible. Since it was man's God-given nature to be tempted to sin at the sight of a woman's body, it was the woman's responsibility to avoid all sexually charged situations.

Christ Commune was not as attractive to women as to men. The women were outnumbered by the men by better than three to one. Over the three years in which the investigators visited the commune they noted that the rigid rules about female members had relaxed somewhat. They were able to dress a bit more comfortably and had been granted at least a small share of power in running the commune. Perhaps as a result of this relaxation, the proportion of female members in the Christ Commune had risen somewhat.

There is really no way of telling whether Christ Commune and its members are typical of the Jesus movement, or even typical of Jesus communes, so it would be premature to try and draw any conclusions about the future of the Jesus movement in general from a single study. But the investigators felt that a group like Christ Commune had a future.

> The successful agricultural operation of Christ Commune is a major reason for our confidence in the group's future. It provides a solid financial basis and furnishes money for missionary work. As funds come in, teams go into new areas to establish houses, which serve as recruitment centers.
>
> Another reason Christ Commune will last is the members themselves. They are alienated from institutional society, and are disinterested in it (except as a pool of

potential converts). They are noncompetitive, anti-intellectual, and other worldly. In short, either by accident or
design they are unlikely to drift back into ordinary society. Christ Commune and the group it serves will be
around for a long time.

If this assessment is correct, then the Jesus movement, while
not heralding the opening of a new millennium as some of its more
enthusiastic supporters had at first claimed, may at least provide
a place of refuge and comfort for a small segment of our society.

The Charismatic
Renewal Movement

I tried to describe a Catholic Charismatic prayer meeting that I had attended to a middle-aged Catholic neighbor. As I told her about how people were speaking in tongues, and uttering prophecies, and performing healing by laying on of hands, she became more and more suspicious. Finally she asked, "Does the pope know about this?"

I told her that meetings of this type, involving large numbers of priests and nuns, were taking place all over the country, often within Catholic institutions. I assumed that the movement must have at least the tacit approval of the church hierarchy.

She agreed that it did, but said, "Well, I probably wouldn't like it."

She probably wouldn't, for the meetings of Catholic Charismatics are not at all like the masses that she was used to attending. Some Catholics have a far stronger reaction. One Catholic mother told me she had stopped her daughter from going to the meetings because she didn't want her associating with a "bunch of religious fanatics and holy rollers." The fact that some of these "fanatics" were priests and nuns, and that the meetings took place in the gymnasium of a Catholic seminary, didn't impress her one bit.

Actually, when compared to a meeting of Jesus People, a Charismatic meeting is the very picture of middle-class respectability. Certainly these people are not "holy rollers." They do not fall on the ground or foam at the mouth. A member of practically any Pentecostal or Holiness church would feel perfectly at home. Indeed, some might feel that the Holy Spirit was not really present, since the manifestations were so restrained. But the important thing about the Charismatic movement is that it is made up largely of Roman Catholics.

The Charismatic meeting that I attended at a seminary in New Jersey was larger than average, but otherwise quite typical. The meeting followed a very modern and quite emotional celebration of the mass. Most of those who had attended mass, and some non-Catholics who wanted to attend the meeting but refused to attend mass, gathered in the gymnasium of the seminary. There were about 200 in the crowd, seated on chairs in a rough semicircle. A couple of people had guitars, and the meeting opened with some hymn singing. After the songs everyone sat quietly for a few moments. Then a gentle murmur started up in the room.

The young man next to me was talking, apparently to himself, but not in English or any other intelligible language. This was speaking in tongues, or glossolalia. Perhaps half the group was engaged in the same activity. After a while there was silence; then someone was "moved" to get up and read a section from the Bible. There was more singing, a bit of banging on tambourines and a few testimonies about how the Holy Spirit had helped that individual during the week.

This went on for about an hour, but there was an air of tension building. Something more dramatic was supposed to happen. After about an hour and a quarter a woman sitting with her eyes closed raised her hands palms upward over her head and began speaking in a loud voice. The words were English, but their meaning was obscure. What was clear is that this was a prophecy. The voice of God or Jesus was supposed to be speaking directly through this woman as a medium. The enigmatic key phrase to the prophecy was, "Participate in the architecture of My Church!" All over the room paper and pens were produced as people wrote down the words. I had noticed this same woman earlier during mass. Even then she had looked rather dazed, as though she was already in a trance. I was struck by the similarity of her appearance, and of the content of her message, to the appearance and message of the traditional spiritualist medium.

The emotional high point of the evening came when the young man who sat next to me burst out chanting in tongues. It was regular and rhythmical, and sounded to me like a Latin chant (although I know no Latin). When he was finished someone else shouted, "Oh, Lord, grant us an interpretation of Your words."

The meeting ended, apparently by general consent, after about two hours. Everyone in the group seemed, if not exhausted, at least pleasantly relaxed. There was a brief meeting for newcomers afterward, which I attended. The leader of the meeting, a Catholic, stressed how the Charismatic movement had strengthened him in his faith, and he assured other Catholics that there was nothing irregular about such meetings. It was the only hint of denominational differences that I had encountered.

There was also a healing ceremony held in the chapel. About thirty people were involved. There was laying on of hands (a practice in which one person places his hands upon the head of the individual who is to be healed), some praying in tongues and a good deal of joyful laughing.

Most of the people who attended the meeting were young—teen-agers or people in their early twenties. They were a respectable-looking though casually dressed group. I was told that most were regular churchgoers, though some had fallen away before becoming involved in the Charismatic movement. Perhaps three quarters of them were Catholic.

The Charismatic movement does not involve a drastic alteration in lifestyle. No one is required to move out to a commune or to become a "one hundred per cent disciple". But in the testimonies at the meeting, and in private interviews afterward, many of the participants said that meetings of this type had become central to their lives, and that since they had begun attending they had changed their entire attitude toward life.

Everyone in or out of the Roman Catholic Church, hostile or sympathetic to it, readily admits that the Church is in trouble. Traditionalists blame the reforms of the Second Vatican Council, liberals blame the traditionalists and most ordinary Catholics do not know who to blame. The Church is not only losing many of its ordinary members to secular society, it is losing some of its most committed members to other religions, such as some of the Jesus groups. Catholics seeking a deeper and more emotional religious experience have often felt forced to go outside of the church structure. Emotional fundamentalist churches, as well as some of the even more unorthodox sects and groups that we are discussing in this book, contain a fair proportion of ex-Catholics.

The Charismatic movement represents a Catholic response to these religious needs. It began in about 1966. According to Kevin and Dorothy Ranaghan, two of the leading spokesmen for the movement, the first to become involved were some faculty members of Duquesne University in Pittsburgh. These faculty members were all devout Catholics but they felt that there was something lacking in their Christian lives. The Ranaghans wrote, "They couldn't quite put their fingers on it but somehow there was an emptiness, a lack of dynamism, a sapping of strength in their lives of prayer and action."

In their search for a more "dynamic" expression of religion, these Catholics developed an interest in the movement called Pentecostalism. Pentecostal refers to the "spiritual gifts," notably healing and speaking in tongues, that were supposed to have descended upon the early Christians on the day of Pentecost. Throughout the history of Christianity, various groups have had differing attitudes toward the importance of such "gifts." In recent years these gifts have been considered relatively unimportant and many lib-

Hundreds of Catholic Charismatics gathered at Garrison, New York, on Pentecost Sunday 1974, for a day of prayer and song.

eral Christians are ready to deny the reality of such gifts altogether. But there has always been a minority of Christians who have believed that such gifts were neither allegorical nor restricted to the ancient church and who have made these gifts the center of their religious involvement.

Various physical manifestations of the Holy Spirit have traditionally been a part of more emotional revival meetings. After the Civil War there was a powerful "holiness movement" among many Protestants. Modern Pentecostalism grew during the early years of this century out of emotional revival meetings held primarily in Los Angeles. Separate Pentecostal churches were established. The Pentecostal movement spread through the nation and is today worldwide. But it was a movement that attracted primarily the poor and uneducated. Most mainstream denominations looked upon Pentecostal churches with barely concealed scorn. They were "storefront churches" full of "holy rollers." The movement was, in short, not really respectable. And if Pentecostalism was not respectable for Protestants, it was unthinkable for Catholics—unthinkable, at least, until the mid-1960s.

The Pittsburgh Catholics began to attend informal prayer meetings with Protestants from Pentecostal and non-Pentecostal denominations. Soon they, too, began to receive "baptism in the Holy Spirit," an intense and overpowering religious experience which, like all religious experiences, is difficult to describe.

But there is a major difference for the Catholic Pentecostals, if not in the experience itself, then at least in the way that they interpret it. When the Jesus People receive baptism in the Holy Spirit, they tend to speak of it as a "new birth," an experience that has completely changed their outlook on life. Catholics, on the other hand, tend to interpret this experience as a reaffirmation of traditional church values from which they had drifted. The difference is an important one, for it keeps Catholic Pentecostals within the church.

In their book *Catholic Pentecostals,* the Ranaghans quote this description of baptism in the Holy Spirit, as experienced by one of the earliest adherents of the movement:

> Talk about a baptism, it was just like I was being plunged down into a great sea of water, only the water was God, the water was the Holy Spirit. . . . All in all it is not a new experience. It is not a revolutionary experience because it reaffirmed all the things which I'd been trying to hold on to for years and to affirm for so many years; my appreciation of scripture, my appreciation of the eucharist, my appreciation of praying and working with other people. The difference is that it seems to me that everything is easier and more spontaneous and comes from within. . . .

While baptism in the Holy Spirit may be the most intense experience of the Charismatic or Pentecostal, speaking in tongues, or glossolalia, is the most spectacular to the outsider and the most common to a participant. There is a good deal of talk among

Charismatics about healing, but stories of miraculous cures appear to be largely secondhand. Speaking in tongues is something that most Charismatics have experienced themselves, and the experience is something that they greatly cherish. Speaking in tongues is also quite common among the Jesus People.

The person speaking in tongues believes that he is indeed speaking in an unknown language, even though neither he nor anyone else is able to understand it. Others who have studied the subject are equally convinced that this is not the case.

In his book *Tongues of Men and Angels,* William J. Samarin, a linguist and anthropologist, states:

> I have tape-recorded and analyzed countless samples of tongues.
>
> In every case, glossolalia turns out to be linguistic nonsense. A person filled by the Holy Spirit does not speak a foreign human tongue, although glossolalists believe that it is the language of the angels. And in all likelihood, he is not "possessed" in any neurological sense. Glossolalia consists of strings of meaningless sounds taken from those familiar to the speaker and put together more or less haphazardly. The speaker controls the rhythm, volume, speed and inflection of his speech so that the sounds emerge as pseudolanguage—in the form of words and sentences. Glossolalia is languagelike because the speaker unconsciously wants it to be languagelike. Yet in spite of superficial similarities, glossolalia is fundamentally not a language.

Samarin contends that anyone can produce a phrase that will pass as glossolalia "if he is willing to drop his inhibitions. The manufacture of nonesence is quite literally child's play." He compares glossolalia to improvisational jazz, saying that it is used to express emotion the way music expresses emotion.

Objections like those raised by Samarin are not new, and they have not the slightest effect upon a person who habitually speaks in tongues. To such a person the tongues are a sign of the operation of the Holy Spirit. He *knows* they are real and meaningful, far more real and meaningful than the cold analyses of a university full of scientists. The power of this experience is most striking in the Charismatic movement, for most of those involved are well-educated people from backgrounds where displays of religious emotionalism are not a tradition.

What does glossolalia sound like? At the prayer meeting I attended I thought it sounded like Latin. I don't know any Latin, but perhaps because I was in a Catholic seminary I was expecting to hear Latin. Samarin cites the following examples of glossolalia that he has collected.

> "Ama conda amus. Keamo deamo no ma diamos.
> Aako mala amos ceamakkaamos boraonba."

During a Charismatic Renewal prayer meeting a young man stops playing the guitar and starts speaking in tongues.

"Ki lada sphona sa naniia shun ka lana moba deseen
vi ladia so boda shan za she lava kadia nonamakaia
pico dada shan veria dada ko camana."

When the movement first began it was generally called the
Catholic Pentecostal Movement, but more recently the name
Charismatic Renewal Movement has been favored, perhaps because the word Pentecostal has been so thoroughly identified with
Protestantism. Charisma means spiritual power given to an individual. Renewal means that these Catholics contend that they are
merely reviving an old Catholic tradition.

The movement had begun among Catholic faculty members,
and at first it spread from university to university. When large
Charismatic meetings were held at Notre Dame University and
Michigan State, the national press, both religious and secular, began
to take notice. One religious paper headlined, "Spiritualists Claim
Gift of Tongues at Exorcism Rites." The Ranaghans complain,
"Soon the story was carried in the public press in the same more or
less garbled fashion. Conclusion-jumping was rampant. Mass hyp-
nosis! Sexual frustration! LSD!" As the movement grew, however,
it began to receive a generally respectful treatment from the press.

Just how many are involved in the Charismatic Renewal Movement is really impossible to say, for the movement has never really
been organized and has grown in a completely informal manner.
Although major Catholic Charismatic centers exist at the University of Michigan and at Notre Dame University, little Charismatic
groups meeting in private homes throughout the country are the
basic strength of the movement. A fair guess might be that several
hundred thousand people are involved, with maybe one hundred
thousand deeply involved. Not all of those who attend Charismatic
prayer meetings are Catholics. The earliest prayer meetings were
made up of Catholics and Pentecostal Protestants, and the movement has retained that character. Sometimes it sounds as though
the movement itself is on its way to forming its own denomination.

Jesus Peace, a newspaper of the Charismatic movement published in New Jersey, described a major camp meeting of East
Coast Charismatics this way:

Ten thousand of God's people had gathered to lift
Jesus higher. They had gathered together from St. Louis
to New York, not as "Charismatic Presbyterians," nor
"Catholic Pentecostals," nor as "Jesus People." They had
gathered as THE BODY OF CHRIST. Not once during
the entire weekend did we ever hear denominational riff-
raff. Not once did we hear people talking "church!" Peo-
were talking Jesus and living as church.

Some Charismatics are even forming their own communities.

Yet leading Catholic Charismatics continually stress that their
movement is entirely within the Roman Catholic Church. Prayer
meetings are often held after mass. They repeat that baptism in
the Holy Spirit, and evidence of the various gifts, in no way makes
them more holy than the average good Catholic who merely at-
tends mass and does not speak in tongues. Still, one can hardly
imagine that this vigorous but unorthodox movement, led entirely
by laymen, makes the traditional Catholic hierarchy entirely comfortable. My own impression from talking to young Charismatics,
Catholic and non-Catholic, was that they had a greater identifi-
cation with the movement than with the churches into which they
had been born. In a September 1974 report on the Charismatic
movement the *New York Times* said that leaders of the movement
were becoming less apologetic and more militant, and talked openly
of reforming the Church.

John B. Snook, professor of religion at Barnard College believes,
however,

> . . . there is little reason to predict that a sectarian
> development is inevitable among them [the Charis-
> matics]. Many find that traditional liturgy has been trans-
> formed for them into a rich and vital experience, even
> when the service has not been modernized. . . . What
> continues to move them is a clearly religious experience
> with an honored tradition in the Church. So long as the
> Church provides a milieu for such experience and allows
> it to be defined as Catholic, it will provide a real answer
> to a contemporary need.

The Unification Church

For a brief period in September 1974, the most familiar face in Manhattan belonged to the Reverend Sun Myung Moon. Posters with Reverend Moon's picture advertised a speech he was to give in Madison Square Garden on September 18 and seemed to fill every available wall and empty window. Leaflets containing the same photograph of Reverend Moon and also advertising his rally were politely but persistently thrust upon all passers-by by a corps of volunteers. The same face looked out at readers from full-page newspaper ads. The meeting was widely advertised on radio and television.

The publicity blitz worked. Reverend Moon's appearance became a major news event. When the day of the rally came, crowds lined up early, and the Garden was filled to overflowing. True enough, the tickets had been free. But New Yorker's are a blasé lot, and it takes something unusual to get thousands of them to turn out even for a free event.

Unfortunately, the spectacle wasn't as exciting as many had hoped, and better than half of the audience of 20,000 simply walked out during the Reverend Moon's two-hour speech. The boredom of the event was heightened by the fact that Reverend Moon, a Korean, speaks little English, and his words had to be translated. Even the Reverend Moon's active delivery, which includes hand claps, stamps, kicks, and yells, only embarassed many in the audience. But for those who missed it or left early, they too could get the message. For the Moon speech was printed in full in the next morning's *New York Times,* not in the news columns but as an advertisement. It covered two full pages of closely set type.

So by one grandiose publicity stroke Reverend Moon's Unification Church was catapulted from an obscure sect to one of the best known unorthodox religions in America, and the Reverend Moon himself became one of the most controversial religious figures around.

The Reverend Moon's movement has existed for some years, but only recently has he begun to make an impact in America.

Sun Myung Moon was born in 1918 in North Pyongan province, in what was to become North Korea. He had been a Presbyterian, and had studied electrical engineering in Japan. When he was about seventeen years old, he says, he began receiving revelations from God which laid bare the "true meaning" of God's "coded message" in the Bible. Through these revelations he developed a new body of knowledge called the Divine Principles. It was another decade, however, before Moon began preaching his Divine Principles. And when he did, he immediately got into trouble with the new Communist regime in North Korea, and landed in a prison camp. He was freed by UN troops during the Korean War and emigrated south, where he began gathering followers in Seoul, the capital of South Korea. But even here he was not free from trouble and controversy.

His movement was attacked by regular Korean Christians. There were persistent rumors that Reverend Moon engaged in ritual sex with his female followers. Ultimately he was arrested for adultery and draft dodging. Today Moon's followers say the charges were false and stress that none of them was ever proved and that he was acquitted. Reverend Moon's relations with the South Korean government have also improved tremendously—so much so that there are now charges that he is actually an agent of that government, charges which are also vigorously denied.

After gathering a devoted and disciplined band of followers in Korea, Reverend Moon began to expand his movement by sending missionaries out to other lands and going on speaking tours. The movement has been quite successful in Japan, less so in other Asian countries. Accurate figures on just how many followers the Reverend Moon has worldwide are hard to come by. Estimates range anywhere from 300,000 to three million. The largest number still appears to be in South Korea.

Reverend Moon did not begin his mission in the United States until 1972, when he made his first speaking tour. At that time he did not attract a great deal of attention, and rarely gathered crowds of more than a few hundred. But even at this early stage of his American expedition, Reverend Moon appeared to have both more money and more influence than the leader of an unorthodox religion usually has. Indeed, it was difficult at first for the outsider to see just how unorthodox Reverend Moon really was.

His followers are always well-dressed and well-groomed. His literature, with the inevitable picture of Reverend Moon, shows him wearing a dark suit and narrow tie. The literature speaks vaguely of a "New Opportunity for Christianity." During the last months of former President Richard Nixon's Watergate crisis, Moon sponsored full-page ads in major newspapers proclaiming GOD LOVES NIXON. His followers held a series of demonstrations in Washington, D.C., in which they prayed for Nixon and all the members of the House and Senate. Reverend Moon himself visited the White House and was photographed with the former President. All in all, he looked like a fairly standard, conservative evangelist who happened to have been born in Korea.

That impression, however, is extremely misleading, for as Reverend Moon has often told his followers, "We are not ordinary Christians." Indeed they are not, and many critics of the movement claim that they are not Christians at all.

One of the revelations received by Reverend Moon was that it had been God's original plan to have Adam and Eve marry and have perfect, sinless children, who would multiply and dwell forever in an earthly paradise. But, says Moon, because of Satan's intervention this plan miscarried. "Under the false fatherhood of Satan, Adam and Eve united as a couple unlawfully, without God's blessing or permission." The result was that all of the descendants of Adam and Eve became literally children of Satan, and that Satan is the real master of this world.

The career of Jesus, according to Reverend Moon's Divine Principles, is another of God's failures. Jesus was sent among the Jews as the Messiah, but the Jews failed to recognize him, and thus he was crucified by mistake. "Jesus did not come to die," says Reverend Moon.

This doctrine angers many Christian clergymen and Moon's critics say that it simply disqualifes him from being a Christian. "The heart of Christianity is that Christ died for the sins of the world," the Reverend Paul Moore, pastor of the Manhattan Church of the Nazarene and a severe critic of Reverend Moon, told the *New York Times*. "He denies the basic tenet of the Christian faith."

Yet the most controversial part of Reverend Moon's Divine Principles does not concern his interpretation of Christianity's past, but his predictions for Christianity's future. He preaches that the world as we know it is in the "last days," and that a new Messiah is about to come, or may already be on earth just waiting to be recognized. And who is that new Messiah to be? Reverend Moon isn't saying exactly, but it is impossible to escape the impression that his followers believe that he is the Messiah—and he does not actively seek to contradict the impression.

Moon has said that this new Messiah, this Third Adam, will be a man, born in Korea in this century. The new Messiah will become the father of a Perfect Family that will redeem mankind and begin the millennium. Reverend Moon is married for the second time (for the fourth time according to his critics) and has seven children.

Marriage is very important to Moon's movement. In 1970 he attracted attention in Seoul by conducting a mass wedding for 793 couples. He is said to be planning another mass wedding in

America. The church must approve any marriage plans of a member. But church spokesmen deny that they arrange marriages. Sex outside of marriage is not allowed.

At one time Reverend Moon appears to have preached that the Koreans were to play the role of "the Chosen People" of the twentieth century. More recently however, he has laid more stress on America and Americans. Reverend Moon himself now spends much of his time in America, where he has a permanent resident's visa. He lives on a large estate near Tarrytown, New York.

The followers of Reverend Moon's Unification Church are devoted and hard-working. Ideally, the believer is expected to surrender all of his or her wealth, retaining only enough to survive while working for the movement. Members can either work at conventional jobs, and turn over the bulk of their wages to the church, as well as spend most of their nonworking hours in missionary effort; or they can work full-time for the church, and have their needs taken care of by the church. In the United States deeply committed members live in communal centers scattered throughout the country.

In some parts of the world, missionary work for the Unification Church can be a wrenching endeavor. One South Korean missionary related:

> "My husband and I have been pioneering in different provinces, and to do this we had to send our four children into orphanages. I climb to a mount every day and gather brush and wood to make bundles of fuel to carry down to a village and sell. With the money I buy a few pounds of oats for my living. Supporting myself in this way, I proclaim the truth day after day and month after month."

In preparing for the Manhattan rally, the industriousness of Moon's young followers, or the Moon children as they were often called, became almost legendary. About 1,000 of them were brought to New York to help publicize the event. Many were Americans, but there were also numerous Koreans, Japanese and individuals from other countries.

After they had put up the huge number of posters, the city government told them that placing advertising on public property was illegal, and that they were going to be fined up to $10 a poster. The total would have been staggering, but also difficult to collect, since illegal posters are put up on public property all the time, and the worst offenders are usually candidates for public office. Yet at dawn on the morning following the rally Moon's followers were out carefully removing all of the illegal posters. They could not have had more than a few hours' sleep, if that. When a reporter asked them if they were tired, one replied that this life was for working and not for sleeping. Indeed, Moon's followers appear to glory in the severity of the lives that they have chosen to lead.

There have been charges that Moon's disciples are undernourished and so severely overworked that they are often ill. But there was no evidence of this in the volunteers passing out literature on the streets. They looked well-fed, alert, and unflaggingly enthusiastic.

The majority of Moon's American followers appear to be middle-class, white, and in their late teens or early twenties. His spokesmen assert that intensive recruiting campaigns on college campuses produces the largest number of converts. The Moon children are, in short, very much the same type of individuals who are attracted to many other current unorthodox religions.

If a young convert's parents object and try to block their child's involvement in the movement, the converts are then advised to break off relations with them. In 1967 a group of Korean parents formed an organization similar to FREECOG in America. It was devoted to getting their children from under Reverend Moon's control, and to exposing the Unification Church. Parents charged that their children had been "hypnotized" or "brainwashed" and made "prisoners" of the moment. A similar organization was formed in Japan and held public demonstrations in front of Moon's headquarters. The same sort of charges have followed the expansion of Reverend Moon's movement in America.

There is nothing unique or unprecedented about Reverend Moon's philosophy or his apparent claim to be the new Messiah.

Reverend Sun Myung Moon addresses the crowd at his Madison Square Garden rally.

Self-proclaimed messiahs are hardly unfamiliar figures on the religious scene in this or any other era. Nor are the charges of sexual promiscuity, brainwashing, and exploiting deluded followers new. Similar charges have been leveled against practically every leader of an unorthodox religion. But there are two things about Moon's Unification Church which are a bit unique, and they concern money and politics.

Clearly the Unification Church has a great deal of money. The cost of the Madison Square Garden extravaganza, including the publicity, has been estimated as high as half a million dollars. Even if that estimate is exaggerated, it is obvious that Reverend Moon was able to spend far more on a one-day rally than Billy Graham spends on a crusade which lasts a week or more. Nor is the Madison Square Garden rally a one-shot affair. Reverend Moon is planning similar appearances in other cities. Since its beginning, Reverend Moon's movement has been marked by periods of intense missionary activity.

Then there is the property that the church owns. According to the *New York Times* Reverend Moon's estate in Tarrytown cost an estimated $850,000. It serves as international center for the movement as well as Moon's primary home, and is tax-exempt. Farther up the Hudson there is another church estate purchased from the Christian Brothers for a reported $625,000. There are also a half dozen or so centers around the New York area where members of the Unification Church live and work. And these are just the church's New York State holdings.

Little is known of Reverend Moon's personal lifestyle. He no longer grants interviews to reporters, and even a few years ago when he did he appeared stiff and formal and not very informative. In public appearances he dresses conservatively, and is said by his supporters to be a hard worker. He claims to take no money from the church, but he is president or director of church-owned businesses, so his personal fortune and that of his church are really inseparable.

Where is all the money coming from? Church spokesmen say that the funds for the American evangelization campaign came from a large interest-free loan from the Unification Church in Japan, where it is well-established. The bulk of the funds for running the church on a day-to-day basis comes from what members raise through operating a few small businesses, and from street sales of peanuts, candles, flowers and dried-flower arrangements. One former member of the Unification Church told a *New York Times* reporter that she could make over $100 a day on street sales and simply by asking for donations.

Yet the suspicion persists that all of that money cannot come simply from peanut sales and austere living. And that leads to the second unusual aspect of the Unification Church: its possible political involvement.

When the church first began to grow in South Korea the government looked upon it with extreme disfavor, and Reverend Moon was arrested. But Reverend Moon adopted a vigorous anti-Communist stance which fit well with the official government position, and the government's attitude began to change. In recent years the South Korean government has jailed not only political opponents, but many clergymen as well. President Chung Hee Park of South Korea has assumed near-dictatorial powers, and has been sharply criticized by clergymen in and out of Korea for many of his actions. Yet in this increasingly repressive atmosphere Reverend Moon's cause has flourished, and church-owned businesses in Korea have prospered as well. Many of these businesses, like the church's titanium plant, could not operate at all without a government license. Most of the employees in these plants are church members who receive only token wages for their hard work. Thus the businesses can be immensely profitable.

Critics also point out that Reverend Moon's translator and chief associate is Colonel Bo Hi Pak, a former Korean Army officer who was military attaché in Washington from 1961 to 1964. Colonel Pak says that he has no connection whatever with the South Korean government today.

Another charge made by critics is that in South Korea members of the Unification Church have often used violent tactics against their opponents. In the United States some clergymen who have led the opposition to Reverend Moon say they have been harassed by threatening phone calls. Church spokesmen flatly deny both charges, and insist that they are the ones who are being persecuted. Some of the criticism, they say, appears to be "Communist-inspired."

But Reverend Moon's followers do not appear to view the world in primarily political terms. Rather they see everything as part of the basic struggle between the forces of God and the forces of Satan. John Lefland of the University of Michigan has written, in an analysis of the movement:

> All events in the material world are caused by the actions of spirit persons in one or the other of the two camps. Persons in the spirit world cause events in the material world for a purpose related to this cosmic bat-

tle. Satan's spirits hinder and God's spirits help those in the material world who help God (in the form of the Divine Principles movement). Satan's spirits help and God's spirits hinder those who help Satan (which means all who oppose the Divine Principles movement).

This conception provides believers with a simple and powerful scheme for interpreting the "meaning" of everyday events: anything that hinders or hurts the believer, the movement, or those aligned with it, is an attack by Satan's spirits; anything that helps a believer, the movement, or those aligned with it, is an act of helping or leading by God's spirits. Through constant application of this scheme in everyday life, members come to have an immediate and close sense of unseen forces operating on the physical order (for example, the weather) and intervening in world affairs, in relations among nations, in the latest national disaster, and in their own daily lives. Missed or caught buses, cars breaking down or running smoothly, poor and good health, missed and kept appointments, chance and arranged meetings, lost and found property—everything and anything—belongs to a world of spirit casuality.

None of this is basically very different from the attitude of members of other religious groups, particularly fundamentalist Christians. But members of the Unification Church do appear to press this view of casuality with more intensity than most others.

Many people find such a view appealing. It gives simplicity and meaning to life which often seems overly complex and meaningless. Life is further simplified for Moon's followers by the fact that all major decisions, like where they are to go and what they are to do, are made for them by Reverend Moon or his close associates. Independent thought is not encouraged, or perhaps even tolerated. "I am your brain," Reverend Moon has reputedly told his followers. This, of course, is entirely consistent with a theology in which Moon is the Messiah. He is directly expressing God's will, and to obey him is to obey God. To fight his enemies is to fight the servants of Satan.

Even the austere conditions of life imposed by Reverend Moon upon his followers have an appeal. Life is stripped to its absolute essentials. There is only one purpose—spreading "the truth." Whatever hardships they encounter now will be more than made up for in the very near future when "the truth" of Reverend Moon's Divine Principles becomes obvious to all. Then the kingdom of God will be established here on earth, and those who saw "the truth" early will become virtual demigods. The masses who remained unconverted or who actually opposed God's plan will be brought before them for judgment.

Again, there is nothing really new in this appeal. It is the same appeal that millennial movements have always had. The major difference is that for the Moon children this millennial view is a very active part of their day-to-day lives.

Despite all its manufactured publicity, though, Reverend Sun Myung Moon's Unification Church still has a relatively small number of followers in America, though church spokesmen insist that the number of converts is growing rapidly.

The future of Reverend Moon's movement is, of course, impossible to predict. Lefland believes that "movements like the Divine Principles have an important function in developing countries. They can transform a passive belief in the natural and inevitable character of whatever exists into a faith that things can be changed —by God, man, or both."

The United States is not a developing country. However, in recent years many people, particularly young people, appear to be afflicted by a sense of helplessness and hopelessness. The traditional American faith in progress and our capacity to solve problems has been severely damaged. The ability of the Reverend Moon to inspire his followers with a strong sense of purpose, and of power, should not be underestimated.

Section Two

Eastern Religions

The Divine Light Mission

The first thing that strikes an outsider about the Guru Maharaj Ji is that this chubby teen-ager from India is a pretty unlikely looking god. And he says the most outrageous things, in a nasal, rather petulant voice. He compared the gift of Divine Knowledge to getting a Superman comic book. When asked an embarrassing question he snapped, "What do you want from me. I'm just a fifteen-year-old kid."

The sheer improbability of it all accounts in large measure for the Guru Maharaj Ji's spectacular rise to fame, and quite possibly fortune, in America over the last few years.

One disciple, or "premie" as they are called, of the Guru's Divine Light Mission told me she was first attracted to the movement because she couldn't figure out how a kid (he was thirteen at the time she first heard of him) could have millions of followers. Another devotee told an interviewer that the Guru couldn't be a con artist because he just did too bad a job of it. A good con artist, the disciple reasoned, wouldn't wear a gold watch or give such stupid answers to questions.

The Guru Maharaj Ji's first trip to America took place in 1971. At the time he was virtually unknown; only his extreme youth set him apart from the host of other Eastern gurus who have come to America in search of followers.

When Guru Maharaj Ji returned the following year, thousands attended a festival held in his honor in Colorado. By 1973 his followers were able to rent the Astrodome in Houston for a three-day festival at a cost of $25,000 a day. Guru Maharaj Ji and his family stayed in the Celestial Suite of the Astroworld Hotel. The suite normally rents for $2,500 a day, though it is said the Guru got a reduced rate.

In the past, religious leaders have often first attracted wide attention by making a famous convert. This is certainly the case with the Guru Maharaj Ji. It was a conversion somehow symbolic of the times in which we live, for the celebrity convert was not a movie star, or even a rock superstar, but a protest leader. Rennie Davis was one of the most famous (or notorious, depending upon your point of view) of the young radicals of the mid-1960s. Along with Abbie Hoffman, Tom Hayden and four others, Davis was one of "the Chicago Seven" indicted after the disturbances at the 1968 Democratic Convention in Chicago. He had been jailed, beaten and even risked death as one of the most articulate spokesmen against the war in Vietnam.

In January 1971 Davis was flying to Paris to meet with the Vietcong delegation. On the plane he met a film crew going to India to see the Guru Maharaj Ji. He was skeptical but intrigued by what they told him, so he decided to go to India and see for himself.

"The thing that triggered my fancy," he explained, "was that you didn't need faith; the whole thing was an experience. That's what attracted me about the New Left, the rejection of dogma and the approach by process. Guru Maharaj Ji said, 'Don't believe me unless you have proof.' " Davis went to India, and got his proof. "It really gave me grace and moved me into a suppression of time and space."

"Ever since I've returned from India," he said, "I've felt the hope, the incredible joy which I think can await us all. I have realized that the hopes of the Sixties are going to be fulfilled in the Seventies, that the Sixties' generation of peace is going to finally peak. . . ."

Many of the Guru Maharaj Ji's followers were, or could have been, followers of Rennie Davis in the 1960s. But many others in and around the New Left have viewed Davis' conversion with a mixture of incredulity and rage. Says Davis, "I remember last spring when I traveled around the country announcing to old friends the joyous news. Many of them thought I had lost my mind or was secretly working for the CIA. I spoke in Berkeley and New York and said, 'The Creator has come to help us pull the world back together again,' and tomatoes and cherry pies were hurled at me."

When Davis debated Paul Krassner, editor of the radical publication *The Realist,* Krassner was unusually bitter and compared the appearance of the Guru to the "second coming of Santa Claus." Abbie Hoffman, Davis' codefendant in the Chicago trial, said of the Guru, "If this guy is God then he is the god that the United States of America deserves."

Controversial is perhaps the mildest adjective one might use to describe the Guru Maharaj Ji.

In mid-1974 Julie Cooper, a premie who handles press relations for the New York City office of the Guru's Divine Light Mission, estimated that some 60,000 Americans had received Knowledge (the term will be explained shortly) in accordance with the rules laid down by the Guru. She estimated that anywhere from 5 to 10 per cent of these were living in communal centers called ashrams. There are about fifty ashrams scattered through the country. Julie herself, like most of the others who work for the DLM, lives in an ashram, and devotes full time to the Guru's cause, or "doing service," as they call it.

In addition, the Guru is said to have over six million followers worldwide. The vast majority of these are in India, but a fair number are in England and other parts of Europe. And, Julie proudly pointed out, the Guru is still only sixteen years old.

The figures are uncheckable, and DLM officials admit that their records are not very good. But at least for America, the number of devotees may not be greatly exaggerated. Unquestionably the Guru Maharaj Ji is the center of one of the fastest growing religions in America today.

The Guru's followers have produced a film, a book and a series of lectures all entitled "Who is Guru Maharaj Ji?" Well, who is he?

The Guru Maharaj Ji was born in Hardwar, India, on December 10, 1957. He was the youngest of three sons of Shri Hans Ji Maharaj, himself a famous guru, or teacher, in India and in the view of his followers the previous Satguru, or Perfect Living Master. According to the Divine Light Mission, Christ and Buddha were Satgurus in their own time. Shri Hans Ji, who had come from a wealthy family, spent much of his life preaching among the poor. "The world is for the wealthy, but God is for the poor," he had said. Shri Hans Ji died, or as his followers prefer to put it, shed his body in 1966, but not before passing leadership in his movement on to his youngest son. Guru Maharaj Ji was only thirteen at the time, but already recognized as the new incarnation of the Perfect Master.

The young Perfect Master was, and still is, aided by his mother, Shri Mata Ji, and his three older brothers. They are known collectively as the Holy Family, and any one of them commands almost as much respect from premies as does the Guru himself.

Guru Maharaj Ji and his relatives expanded the movement not only in India but well beyond its borders. He does not appear to place the same emphasis on the poor as God's chosen people as did his father. In the West at least, the movement is almost entirely middle-class. The Guru has said that in India people are often physically hungry, whereas in the West they are spiritually hungry.

Do the followers of this teen-aged Guru worship him as God? They are extremely hesitant to say so. "I'd rather not get into that," Julie Cooper told me. "The word God has too much emotive meaning. Everybody has his own idea of God, and you are going to get the wrong impression if I say that he is God."

When a reporter in Houston asked the Guru, "Are you the son

The teen-aged Perfect Master, Guru Maharaj Ji, addresses a mass gathering of his followers in India.

of God?" the answer he received was, "Everybody's the son of God. You ain't the uncle or aunt of God, are you?"

Yet the conclusion that the Guru's followers do indeed regard him as God is inescapable. Divine Light Mission offices are decorated with his picture. Many of the devotees wear large buttons adorned with his portrait. In his presence they virtually lay their heads at his feet. Those who have seen him or heard him describe how totally overwhelming and supernatural the experience is.

When not being coy with reporters the Guru Maharaj Ji makes some definitely God-like pronouncements.

> If you do not obey what the Maharaj Ji says, what is the use of your living in this world? Rather you should die

of shame! No Guru Maharaj Ji has come. Whenever he
came before you did not accept Him. Now I have come
again to reveal the Knowledge, and still you do not understand me. . . . The great leaders think that I have
come to rule and yes, they are right! I will rule the
world, and just watch how I will do it!

The Guru Maharaj Ji stands at the apex of an elaborate worldwide organization called the Divine Light Mission. The DLM was
begun by the Guru's father in 1960. By 1973 it claimed to have
480 centers in thirty-eight countries. Aside from the centers themselves there are a wide variety of subsidiaries. Shri Hans Productions makes films, Shri Hans Records presses recordings, Shri Hans
Publications produces newspapers and magazines. There are also
an educational service, a health service, a travel service, an airline,
an electronics firm and a theater group. Some of these subsidaries
appear to have ceased functioning by mid-1974, or may have existed in name only. Still, the list remains an impressive one.

Much criticism has been leveled against the Royal Family's opu-
lent lifestyle. The contrast is particularly striking when one realizes
that most of the premies in ashrams live austerely. But the premies
don't seem to mind the contrast. One told a reporter who questioned him about the Guru's Rolls Royce, "Do you expect him to
ride on a donkey?"

Most of the Divine Light Mission's funds in America come from
gifts from followers, or from the wages of those who live in the
ashrams. These full-time workers give free service to the DLM's
many activities, or work in organizations like Divine Services, a
cleaning and repairing organization, or in outside jobs not directly
connected with the DLM. In return they receive lodging and food
in the ashrams. None of those to whom I spoke felt that they were
in any way being exploited, and that full-time service was the least
they could do in the cause of the Living Perfect Master.

The Divine Light Mission has no elaborate theology or philosophy; in fact, neither word is ever used. All holy books—the Bible,
the Koran, the Bhagavad-Gita, etc.—are considered equally valid,
though the Gita gets the most attention, "because it's the oldest,"

I was told, but also, one imagines, because it, like the Divine Light movement, comes from India. But the core of the appeal of the Guru's message is not an idea or a thought but an experience.

Indeed, rational thought, or "mind," is the supreme enemy of the inner peace preached by the Guru. In this respect the Guru Maharaj Ji's message is no different from that of many other Eastern philosophies which stress meditation. Mind is regarded as an obstacle on the road to whatever blissful state the particular religion regards as ultimate, and it is something to be overcome.

The Guru has denounced mind in no uncertain terms. "Do you know, the devil is the son of man that comes to mind, through mind, from mind." Questioning, the Guru has said, "creates terrible suffering in your mind. You cannot sleep at night because of the illusive question."

If the Guru Maharaj Ji offers no intellectual satisfaction, in fact scorns the intellect, what does he offer? The answer is experience: a deeply personal and, to his devotees, entirely overpowering experience which frees one from the "devil" of mind and gives him peace.

Time after time premies stress that the Guru Maharaj Ji or his apostles can give you a concrete experience that will open the universe for you. It is the "proof" of God, of which Rennie Davis spoke. This experience is called receiving Knowledge.

Some Americans received Knowledge by traveling to India, but this is no longer absolutely necessary. The road traveled by Julie Cooper is more typical today. She had been in law school in Florida, but found school, and life in general, unsatisfactory. Then she said she met followers of the Guru, whom she described as "leading real natural lives." She began to attend satsang. Satsang is one of the most important activities of the DLM followers. It means literally the company of truth. Satsang takes place when the Guru, one of his family or any of his followers sit around and talk about the Knowledge, or the Guru, or what it feels like to be a premie. A Christian equivalent to delivering satsang might be giving a sermon or testimony, or even public confession.

While there is no set form for satsang, and each premie has his or her own story to tell, this paragraph is fairly typical:

I was still suspicious, but I was attracted to the Guru and to the energy that was flowing around his devotees. So I stayed at the Carmel [California] ashram where the mahatma was speaking. Then I received Knowledge. After meditating on the Knowledge I can see how this common experience of God can unite all men and bring peace on earth. Guru Maharaj Ji will awaken your sleeping soul and give you peace. Many prophets have come and by their fruits you should judge them. I became a disciple of Guru Maharaj Ji because I know he has the power of God behind him. Since he opened my third eye I have access to eternal peace and can see into the world of the Living Master. The time is coming very shortly when the ways of ignorance and darkness, the way of industrial militarism will be swept away like dust under the feet of the Satguru.

Premies readily admit that printed satsangs do not make particularly exciting reading. But they stress that it is not the words themselves but rather the feelings or "vibrations" an individual gets from hearing satsang delivered that is most important.

Julie Cooper went to New Orleans to receive Knowledge from a mahatma. Knowledge, the central act of the entire Maharaj Ji cult can only be given by a mahatma, an apostle of the Guru. I was told that there are about 2,000 of them in the entire world. The number is relatively small, considering the size of the movement, and there is only a single westerner, an Englishman, who has ever achieved this exalted position. There have never, except for major festivals, been more than four or five mahatmas in all North America. They travel from city to city giving Knowledge to eager would-be premies. One has to catch them on the fly.

Those who have received Knowledge, and are satisfied with it, are reluctant to talk about it, or to do anything but describe the experience in the most general sort of terms. In a Knowledge session a mahatma is supposed to reveal the four techniques of inner meditation, known as Divine Light, Divine Harmony, the Word and Nectar.

Ken Kelly, a journalist who was researching a book on the Divine Light Mission, found some defecting premies who described the Knowledge session in detail. This is his admittedly unfriendly account:

> You are taken into a very dark room, there are no more than fifteen of you. The mahatma is sitting against the middle of a wall with a very bright light on him. First he *satsangs* you for about two hours about the retribution you're going to suffer if you ever reveal the secret of the Knowledge-giving. Fire and brimstone stuff, suffering and gnashing of teeth, eternal damnation. Then he starts giving Knowledge. First he does your eyes. He presses his knuckles very hard upon your eyeballs and keep them there until you see the *light*. Then he plugs up your ears with his fingers in a certain way until you hear the *music*. Then he tips your head back in a certain way for the meditative position, and that *nectar* you taste that's your snot. Then he tells you the secret word to meditate on, and that's a kind of breath sound that's suppose to represent the divine energy of the world, ah-ha, ah-ha.

The techniques are absurdly simple when described in this way. I can easily see the light or at least a light when I press hard on my own eyeballs. It can also be painful, so I don't recommend playing around with the procedure. I can get a strange sound, which might conceivably be called music, by plugging up my ears with my fingers. I have never quite succeeded with the nectar, because it involves putting your tongue back in your throat, and I resist because I'm afraid I'll choke myself, but I have no doubt that it too is easy enough. As far as the word is concerned, a mantra or secret sound is basic to most forms of meditation. Psychologists believe that such a sound, and any nonobjectionable sound will do, simply serves as a focus for attention during meditation.

While the premies will not say the techniques described by Ken Kelly and others are inaccurate, they insist that a mere physical description of the technique is both inadequate and misleading. They say that the light that I or anyone else can see by pressing on his own eyeballs is in no way comparable to the light which one gets in a Knowledge-giving session. An official publication of the Divine Light Mission stresses that "to know the techniques of Knowledge without having the Grace of the Perfect Master is quite useless." Grace, according to official definition, is "The blessings of the Perfect Master. The power which allows us to practice meditation. 'Knowledge without Grace is like a car without petrol,' says Guru Maharaj Ji."

The greatest selling point of the Divine Light Mission is that it can provide a concrete and infallible experience which will give peace and prove that the Guru Maharaj Ji is the Perfect Master. The experience, however, is far from infallible, for there are dropouts and many who ask for Knowledge are never given it.

I pressed Julie Cooper on this point. She said that all one needed to receive Knowledge was a "guileless heart." How, I wondered, did this differ from the claims of many other religious groups which insisted that all one needed to receive their equivalent of Knowledge was to sincerely desire it. For example, many Jesus People claim that if one prays sincerely, one will experience baptism in the Holy Spirit. She simply shrugged and said that if there were other paths to truth that was fine, but why would an individual need more than one Perfect Master? Besides, one could not really compare the experiences, since Knowledge could not be described. She also stressed that in most other religions the divinity was spiritual, but for the DLM the Perfect Master was on earth and accessible to his followers.

But receiving Knowledge isn't the end of the road. Indeed, some of the premies that I talked to found Knowledge an interesting but not overpowering experience. Julie Cooper said that she fell away from the DLM for some six months after receiving Knowledge. For Howard Hershfield, director of the New York office of the DLM, the actual Knowledge session was nothing more than "interesting" or "far out." It wasn't until about half an hour later that he "realized that Knowledge" in what he called "the most profound emo-

Just listening to the Guru Maharaj Ji can be a profound emotional experience for many of his young followers.

tional experience I ever had in my life up to that point." An equally profound emotional experience came to him a few months later when he found the Guru Maharaj Ji standing behind him in an airport.

Premies compare receiving Knowledge to "planting a seed" which must be carefully nurtured in order to continue to grow. The Knowledge techniques are supposed to be used in order to aid the premie in his daily meditations. It is recommended that the premie spend at least two hours a day in meditation, and there are stories of premies who have meditated for twenty-four hours straight. From meditation one is supposed to get peace. I don't really know what is meant by "peace," but I take it to be a blissful inner serenity. Premies also say that in addition to formal meditation, which takes place when they are sitting quietly, they are really meditating all of the time. As they talked to me they said that they were also meditating.

In order to nurture the seed, a percentage of premies move into ashrams. There they live a highly structured, communal, celibate life, eating a vegetarian diet and doing whatever sort of service is required of them. Under such conditions they associate primarily with other premies.

But even then peace does not come automatically. Mark Sharron, a lay therapist who received Knowledge at the age of sixty-five (unusual in a movement that appeals primarily to people under thirty), spends part of his time counseling premies. Often, he says, they are prey to anxieties during meditation, and they become frightened. "But I tell them this is good because they are getting into contact with themselves." Studies of other meditation techniques have indicated that a certain percentage of those who try meditation experience great anxiety and depression. Meditation, say the psychologists, lowers personal defenses and in the case of extremely anxious people leaves them prey to all sorts of fears that would otherwise have been kept under control. For such individuals meditation, any form of meditation, can be harmful and result in a variety of psychological and psychosomatic disturbances. For the majority, however, meditation appears to be both harmless and relaxing. Meditation is also an extremely ancient technique that has been used by Christian mystics in the past.

Ken Kelly, however, sees meditation in a far more sinister light. Says Kelly:

> When the mind cannot answer any of the questions on the road to satori, it is the mind that must be annihilated, not the road that must be re-examined. . . .
>
> Guru Maharaj Ji instills in his followers a mind-control device that would surely make the Central Intelligence Agency envious. Called "The Knowledge," it is a combination of several ancient yoga meditation techniques that members must practice several times a day, and particularly when the mind threatens to reassert its

rational thrust. So when the Guru's ostensible message of peace and love is overshadowed by the violent practice that can accompany it, a follower can purge the mind of all contradictions by meditating them into oblivion.

The "violent practice" that Kelly is talking about is the charge that the Divine Light Mission is implicated in an attempted murder of one of the Guru Maharaj Ji's opponents. On August 7, 1973, Pat Halley, who worked for an underground newspaper in Detroit, hit Guru Maharaj Ji in the face with a shaving cream pie. His reason was, "I always wanted to throw a pie in God's face." The Guru was embarassed, but unhurt.

A week later two men, one an Indian in his mid-fifties, the other a young American, came to Halley's apartment. They said that they were going to "expose" the DLM by showing Halley the hypnotic techniques that were used in the Knowledge sessions. They told Halley to close his eyes, which he did, but instead of showing him how Knowledge was given, they very nearly bludgeoned him to death with a blackjack. For the rest of his life Halley will have to wear a plastic plate in his head to protect the spot where the blows shattered his skull.

The two assailants turned out to be Mahatma Fakiranand, one of the small number of apostles empowered by the Guru himself to give Knowledge, and twenty-five-year-old Richard Fletcher, one of the Guru's earliest and most enthusiastic American converts. Fletcher is also considered to be a reincarnation of St. Peter. The Guru immediately issued a statement which said that the assailants had confessed, and that "the Divine Light Mission wished to help in whatever way possible to see that the persons responsible are brought to justice." Officials of the DLM also said that the pair could not be true devotees, for no true follower of the Guru could perform such an act, and that the pair had been banished from the DLM.

Julie Cooper said that she had been in a Chicago ashram where the two assailants were being held for the police, but the police never came, and so the pair was allowed to leave. Yet far from being severed from the Guru's good graces, Mahatma Fakiranand has gone to Europe where he continues to give Knowledge. The other assailant has also eluded police, who in any case do not seem to be trying very hard to apprehend him.

Followers of the Guru are not unduly upset over this violent incident. Some appear to believe that the whole thing is some kind of gigantic game that the Guru Maharaj Ji is playing in order to test their loyalty. Many others believe that the attack was entirely justified. One premie told a TV interviewer that if he caught someone who had thrown a pie at the Guru, he would "cut his throat on the spot!" "On the spot!" he repeated. Most of all, though, premies pass the incident off as something irrelevant to the message of universal peace brought by the Living Perfect Master.

The high point of the Guru Maharaj Ji's western mission was to be Millennium '73, a giant festival held in Houston's Astrodome in November 1973. Though in many ways the festival was impressive, it is hard to escape the conclusion that it was at best a qualified success and may well have been more of a disaster than members of the DLM are willing to concede. Part of the problem was numbers. Though admission to the Astrodome was free, and the event well-publicized, the crowd inside was never larger than 20,000. Billy Graham had drawn over 60,000 to the same arena.

Guru Maharaj Ji himself suffered from the harsh glare of American publicity. Disciples are not out to challenge the Guru's wisdom, and are happy with parables and paradoxes. Reporters are a different breed altogether. In a rough-and-tumble news conference in Houston the Guru looked evasive, particularly when asked about the Detroit beating. One of his assistants insisted that the reporters drop the subject and move on to more relevant questions. But other questions were not answered to the reporters' satisfaction either. For example, when asked why he didn't sell his Rolls Royce and buy food for the people, the Guru replied, "What good would it do? I could sell it and people would still be hungry. I have only one Rolls Royce."

The premies themselves had a genuine expectation that something tremendous would happen—though no one was quite sure what it would be. There was a serious rumor that a UFO was going to land, and there were even spaces left in the Astrodome parking lot for visiting flying saucers. When told of the possible extraterrestrial visitors, Bal Bhagwan Ji, the Guru's eldest brother, remarked, perhaps ironically, "If you see any, just give them some of our literature."

The much publicized Comet Kohoutek was nearing the vicinity of Earth in November 1973. Many religious organizations were predicting all kinds of world-shaking events because of it. Bal Bhagwan Ji noted that there might be significance in the name Ko (knockout) Hou (Houston) Tek (Texas). But the comet that many had called the comet of the century was a fizzle.

Astrologically speaking, the dates for Millennium '73 were considered highly significant. On November 7, the day before Millennium opened, the moon and the planets of Venus, Pluto and Saturn were at right angles, forming what astrologers call the Grand Cross. The following day the constellation Aquarius rose in the West, meaning to some the dawn of the Aquarian age in the West. On November 1, the final day of Millennium '73, Mercury, the planet of the mind, crossed the equator of the sun, an event that takes place only once every thirteen years. According to an astrologer quoted by the *New York Times Magazine,* "This is the very message of the Guru Maharaj Ji, the mind being gobbled up by the basic life force."

The Guru delivered satsang from a blue velveteen throne 300 feet above the floor of the Astrodome. There were flashing lights, huge television screens projected his image, and his likeness in lights even appeared on the Astrodome's celebrated two-million-dollar scoreboard. Down below, Blue Aquarius, a rock band led by the Guru's portly brother Bhole Ji, wearing a silver lamé tuxedo, played the Guru's theme, "O Lord of the Universe." Theatrically it was a good halftime show. Many, probably most of those in the audience, thought it was a great deal more. "You can't imagine the power that was there," one told me.

And yet when it was all over the premies, who had served as a highly efficient volunteer labor force, had to pack up quickly so that the stadium could be prepared for a professional football game that was to be played the next day. Thus ended what was billed as the "most significant event in the history of mankind."

Julie Cooper admitted a little shyly that Millennium '73 suffered
from what she termed "adolescent enthusiasm." Particularly with
"the business about the UFOs."

Millennium '73 left the DLM with a whopping debt and angry
creditors who were threatening to sue. An East Coast publication
of the group announced in its May 12, 1974, issue:

> The Millennium debt is still dwindling at a steady rate as
> donations and DLM earnings slowly pour in. This time
> is pretty critical because in order to finish negotiation
> on the Guru Puja site [another festival tentatively sched-
> uled for Amherst, Massachusetts] the Millennium debt
> must be paid off. The best thing for all premies at this
> time to do is to make a regular (tax deductible) dona-
> tion each week through their local DUO [Divine United
> Organization, an umbrella organization for the Guru's
> many activities] office.

Bhole Ji's Blue Aquarius band has been disbanded.

The DLM's very slick magazine *And It Is Divine* has been sus-
pended at least temporarily. Premies were told that there was a
warehouse full of magazines that should be distributed before they
were recycled.

Worst of all, perhaps, the world has continued just as before.
There was fighting in the Middle East, famine in Africa, terror in
California and Watergate in Washington. If the millennium—a
thousand years of peace—had actually begun at Houston in November of 1973, it was obvious to very few.

Like many other religious organizations, the Divine Light Mission has a strong end-of-the-world bent. Premies feel that the world
simply cannot continue as it is. But instead of seeing the apocalypse
predicted by many Christians, they see an era of peace brought by
their Perfect Master. The time is near, they say, and according to
Rennie Davis, the Guru Maharaj Ji "slipped in the back door just
in the nick of time." How long the DLM can continue to exist without some cataclysmic and objective proof of the Guru's power is
impossible to predict. It appeared that in the early summer of

1974 the Guru Maharaj Ji's Western mission was in a period of retrenchment if not crisis.

Another imponderable is the effect of the Guru's marriage. On May 19, 1974, the Guru married his secretary, Marilyn Lois Johnson, in a private ceremony at his $80,000 home in Colorado. Because of his age, the Guru had to get special permission to marry from a Colorado judge. The judge commented that the Guru "makes quite a bit of money and he seems quite mature—much older than 16." There have been persistent rumors that the Guru is really a lot older than he admits. His bride was twenty-four. Among his many gifts were an expensive sports car and a cabin cruiser. The event drew a lot of snickers from the national news media.

But it would be wildly premature to conclude that the Divine Light Mission was about to go down in a wave of disenchantment because the world as we know it had failed to end, or because the Guru had married an older woman. In the New York area satsang is still being given in dozens of different locations every week. The ashrams continue to function and new ones are being formed all the time. Premies still run a large vegetarian restaurant near Times Square in the heart of Manhattan. Premies organize everything from art shows to yoga lessons. The devotees of the Guru Maharaj Ji seem well on their way to forming a society of their own. Indeed, one of the fondest hopes of many is the Divine City, to be built under the direction of the Guru himself and peopled with his devotees. Just how real or practical this plan is, is impossible to say; many other sects have dreamed of building their own city. But the premies believe the goal is real.

It is unfair to judge the total impact of the Divine Light Mission by the excesses of Houston, the attack in Detroit or even the Guru's gaudy marriage. It is probably even unfair to judge it by the public personality of the Guru Maharaj Ji himself. Individuals like Joseph Smith, prophet of the Mormons, and Mary Baker Eddy, founder of Christian Science, were accused of being insane, crooked or both, yet they founded viable and ultimately even conservative religions.

Many of today's premies may be spiritual floaters, who drift from one movement to another without ever finding peace and satisfaction. Others, perhaps a substantial number, are made of sterner stuff. They have found in the teachings and practices of the Guru Maharaj Ji a peace and fulfillment that had eluded them in the outside world. By joining an ashram or otherwise spending most of their time with like-minded individuals, they are making a serious commitment to a radically different lifestyle. They are not just "playing around" with a currently fashionable religion.

Because the DLM makes such grand claims, it is an easy target for ridicule. But what critics often overlook is that thousands of people have found, and are finding, inner peace and a new sense of purpose in life in the teaching of the Guru Maharaj Ji.

Transcendental Meditation

Transcendental meditation, or TM, isn't exactly a religion. It's more of a technique. But some form of meditation is basic to most of the Eastern religions now popular in the U.S., as well as to a number of other unorthodox religions. TM is probably the most popular, and certainly the most well-studied, form of meditation in America right now and for this reason it is worth a closer look.

TM is the creation of the Maharishi Mahesh Yogi, a multitalented yogi from India. As a young man, the Maharishi obtained a degree in physics from the University of Allahabad, but he soon abandoned Western science for the spiritual quest of a yogi. He spent two years living in a cave in the Himalayas, and more years wandering through the forests of southern India.

In the mid-1950s the Maharishi gave up the hermit's life to become a missionary. His aim was nothing less than the spiritual regeneration of all mankind. He has traveled the world, not as a barefoot pilgrim but in a jet plane, to spread his message. He has lectured in person to hundreds of thousands, made tevevision appearances seen by millions, and explained his mission in three popular books.

Unfortunately, the Maharishi's message, like that of most mystics, Eastern or Western, does not come across well in the printed word. TM is basically an experience. To those who have not shared the experience, a description can sound murky or even rather pretentious. This paragraph, chosen at random from the Maharishi's *The Science of Being and Art of Living,* is fairly typical of his writings:

> Contemplation on the inner-value of life eventually reveals to the aspirant that the ever-changing world is based on a never-changing element of no-form and no-phenomenon. All forms and phenomena belong to the relative field of existence, whereas that which lies beyond all form and phenomena necessarily belong to a field that is out of relativity.

The Maharishi realized that his message was not going to be easy for westerners to grasp. So he refined the technique of Transcendental Meditation so that it could be taught quickly and simply in a technological society.

The Maharishi's fame in the West grew when he picked up some famous followers. The first were the Beatles, particularly George Harrison. The Beatles had moved from psychedelics to meditation. Their infatuation with the Maharishi, however, did not last. Some of the Beatles were even rather bitter about their experience with him, describing it as "a bad trip." But by that time he was well known. Another famous convert was actress Mia Farrow.

The Maharishi is even more efficient in the use of Western organizational techniques than is the Guru Maharaj Ji. Among the organizations he now controls are the Spiritual Regeneration Movement (SRM), Students' International Meditation Society (SIMS), International Meditation Society (IMS), American Foundation for the Science of Creative Intelligence (AFSCI) and Maharishi International University (MIU). Lectures and courses in TM are offered not only in major metropolitan areas but on college campuses and in many other communities as well.

Like the Guru Maharaj Ji, the Maharishi promises very practical and provable results. But unlike the Guru's Knowledge, TM need not be taught by one of a small number of specially anointed mahatmas. It can be taught by a corps of teachers who have been trained for that purpose. Since in order to transform the entire world millions of teachers would be needed, the Maharishi has reduced even the training of teachers and their helpers to an automatic, almost computer-like procedure. No special Grace of the Master is needed.

In early 1974 the Maharishi's organization in Los Angeles estimated that some 300,000 Americans had learned TM and about 15,000 more enrolled in courses every month. Learning TM is both cheap and easy. For under $100 one gets to attend a short series of lectures about TM, gets a bit of individual instruction in the technique and is given a secret Sanskrit mantra to think about while meditating.

By proper meditation for two twenty-minute periods every day, the Maharishi says, the masses of the world will discover "absolute bliss consciousness," the natural and proper state of mankind.

The mantra is in no sense a magic word. It is an aid to meditation, and its use has been recognized by mystics of all ages and all cultures. An anonymous fourteenth-century English Christian mystic wrote a book called *The Cloud of Unknowing*. It is regarded as one of the finest works of Christian mysticism. In it the author describes the use of the mantra, though that is not what he calls it:

> If you want to gather all your desire into one simple word that the mind can retain, choose a short word rather than a long one. A one-syllable word such as "God" or "love" is best. But choose one that is meaningful to you. Then fix it in your mind so that it will remain there come what may. This word will be your defense in conflict and in peace. Use it to beat upon the cloud of darkness above you and subdue all distractions,

consigning them to the cloud of forgetting beneath you. Should some thought go on annoying you, demanding to know what you are doing, answer with this one word alone. If your mind begins to intellectualize over the meaning and connotations of this little word, remind yourself that its value lies in its simplicity. Do this and I assure you these thoughts will vanish. Why? Because you have refused to develop them with arguing.

In America the Maharishi's popularity went into decline a bit after he was dropped by the Beatles. Those normally interested in Oriental religions had never liked him anyway. To long-time students of Yoga or Zen the Maharishi was too deliberately and consciously modern and Western. The big corporation-style organization and aggressive recruitment did not fit in well with the simplicity and detachment that are supposed to be the hallmarks of the traditional holy man. Worst of all in the eyes of these critics, TM itself seemed a cheap and superficial method of attaining serenity. If it could be learned so easily, they assumed that there must be something wrong with it. But most people in the West are not serious students of Oriental religion, and to many the fact that the Maharishi tailored his technique to Western need was very appealing.

Then in 1970 TM got a huge boost from a most unexpected source—science. For some years scientists had been investigating yogi and Zen meditators. Using various monitoring devices they had discovered that there was a measurable and massive difference between an individual in a meditative state and the same individual while he was just sitting quietly. The meditators were profoundly, almost astonishingly relaxed. Moreover, there seemed to be differences in the brain-wave patterns of meditators and nonmeditators, indicating that meditation was more than just relaxing, that it was indeed an altered state of consciousness as the meditators had claimed.

Interesting as such findings might be, they had little apparent significance for the West since both yogi and Zen meditators had to

Maharishi Mahesh Yogi

go through years of rigorous training and isolation. Such a lifestyle would not attract many converts in Western society.

Then scientists decided to test individuals trained in TM, precisely because TM was so easy to learn and tailored specifically for Western needs.

In the March 27, 1970, issue of the prestigious magazine *Science,* the official publication of the American Association for the Advancement of Science, there was an article entitled "Physiological Effects of Transcendental Meditation," by Robert Keith Wallace of the Department of Psychology, School of Medicine Center for the Health Sciences, Los Angeles, California. The abstract of the article reads:

> Oxygen consumption, heart rate, skin resistance, and electroencephalograph measurements were recorded before, during and after subjects practiced a technique called transcendental meditation. There were significant changes between the control period and the meditation period in all measurements. During the meditation, oxygen consumption and heart rate decreased, and the electroencephalogram showed specific changes in certain frequencies. These results seem to distinguish the state produced by transcendental meditation from commonly encountered states of consciousness and suggest that it may have practical applications.

That started the ball rolling. There followed a whole variety of reports, some scientific, some not-so-scientific, about how TM reduced tension, lowered blood pressure, made people more organized and creative, got them off drugs, allowed them to give up smoking, etc. In general the popular press came to treat TM with a respect not generally accorded spiritual disciplines from the East. The effects of TM could apparently be measured, and if we Westerners have faith in anything it is in measurement.

But there were cautionary notes as well. One slightly disturbing element was that experimenters who already believed in the value of TM got consistently better results than experimenters who didn't care much about TM. Wallace, who wrote the article for *Science*, was himself a meditator and has since gone on to become president of the Maharishi International University. This isn't to suggest that his results were in any way faked. They have, to a degree, been confirmed by other experimenters. It merely suggests that the technique of TM alone may not account for the results. Perhaps the atmosphere of an experiment conducted within a company of like-minded individuals helps to produce the more dramatic results. This sort of effect is not uncommon in medical and psychological research—and the researcher is often at great pains to decide what percentage of the results are due to the technique under investigation, and what to other factors that are part of the general atmosphere in which an experiment takes place.

The total impact of research on TM is that it has demystified the subject to a certain extent.

Leon S. Otis and his associates at the Stanford Research Institute divided a group of sixty-two volunteers into meditators and controls. The meditators learned TM. Some of the controls just sat quietly for two periods each day; others sat quietly and repeated a "mock mantra," a simple nonobjectionable sound, but not the secret Sanskrit mantra of TM. A third group made no change in their daily routine.

After three months the meditators reported significant improvements in their lives, everything from more restful sleep to greater creativity. The results were so impressive that most of the controls took up TM after they had finished their part of the experiment. But a long psychological questionnaire indicated that TM did not produce any basic alteration in the personality of the meditators.

Otis also reported that "The controls who simply relaxed twice daily for 15 or 20 minutes, using no mantra at all or repeating a mock mantra, found comforts in the experience that did not differ significantly from what the meditators found."

If the actual experience of meditation did not feel significantly different from simply sitting quietly, why was it that the meditators believed that their lives had improved, while the nonmeditators who just sat had no such relief? The answer, Otis believes, lies in the fact that those who undertook the TM training expected more from it than did the controls who were just sitting.

Harvard psychologist Gary Schwartz believes that expectations hold the key to the success and popularity of a technique like TM:

> A person's beliefs can be crucial to the way he experiences something. The difference between "relaxation," for instance, and "depression" may depend in part of one's expectations. Meditators hope, believe and expect that TM will be a good thing. It's *supposed* to be a good thing, and the supposition helps define the eventual experience.
>
> We have to remember that the meditative state is self-induced, that people are seeking changes in consciousness and can predict more or less what the changes will be. The fact that meditators control the experience almost insures that it will seem worthwhile.

But not everybody finds the experience of meditation a pleasant one. In the Stanford Research Institute study a considerable number of people abandoned TM entirely. Writes Otis, "Those who quit meditating . . . seem to fall into two categories: People with problems too serious to respond to a technique as mild as TM and people whose personalities are already too well-integrated." The extremely anxious individuals found that "the deep calm of mantra meditation 'liberates' nothing but problems." On balance, however, Otis felt that a technique like TM helps more people than it hurts.

But the promises made for TM—for example, that it provides a "solution to all problems" as one TM brochure states—are not borne out by research. Moreover, too much meditation may be harmful to your health. Says psychologist Schwartz:

> For just as too much activity and stress can interfere with the proper functioning of the human animal, I would predict that too much meditation can also harm

the organism. The nervous system needs reasonably intense and varied external stimulation and there is no evolutionary, ethological or biological precedent for massive and prolonged meditation. A few people, with a tendency toward mental illness, may even aggravate their condition by meditating for long periods. . . .

Thus, some of those who have a reputation for meditating for hours or even days on end may not be saintly; they may be quite sick.

Most of the hundreds of thousands who take up TM today tend to look upon it as a relaxing interlude in a busy day. A small percentage of those who have taken up TM have chosen to pursue their studies further. This involves withdrawing from normal day-to-day life and living with like-minded devotees in ashrams either in the U.S. or Europe. But the key to the appeal of TM is that it does not require this kind of total commitment. It does not even require that the student make an attempt to understand the Maharashi's metaphysics, which are drawn from ancient Indian Brahminism.

The Maharish himself encourages both approaches. He appears to be in complete and personal control of the whole TM movement. If one simply wishes to meditate for two twenty-minute periods a day, that is fine. If one wishes to go farther and devote one's entire life to spiritual development and spreading the gospel of meditation, that is so much the better. This extremely practical approach sets the Maharishi apart from many other Eastern gurus who have tried to preach their messages to the West. But there are dangers in this practical approach.

Eventually, one wonders if the metaphysics will not be entirely overtaken by the technology of TM. Already TM supporters tend to talk in the language of psychology and biology rather than in the language of Hindu philosophy. One meditator, Major General Franklin M. Davis of the Army War College, is not trying to achieve the "absolute bliss consciousness" preached by the Maharashi. He has found that the practice of TM "helped me in dealing with people, improved my disposition, and brought my blood pressure down."

While TM is popular on college campuses, and has a wide following among the young, it also attracts a large percentage of older and more conservative people who are not looking for new consciousness or major changes in life. Colin Campbell, an editor of the magazine *Psychology Today*, has described the appeal of TM this way:

> It not only promises salvation, it comes with clear instructions. It's practical. It allows transcendence without alienation. It has credentials from the scientific community. . . . As a result, TM may have the appeal of a powerful little machine available to anyone, like a desktop calculator or a pistol. TM is an equalizer, a humbler of the mighty and uplifter of the weak.

All of this, however, raises an important question. It seems fairly well established that many of the benefits that flow from TM, be they spiritual or physical, depend upon what the meditator expects. Stripped of its metaphysics, and reduced to just another relaxing technique, a bit like counting sheep, the benefits of TM may melt away. It is entirely possible that meditation, in order to be really effective, to be a truly transcendental experience, must be supported by a system of beliefs that are not natural to Western society. To try to explain them in the language of modern science, to make the system consciously modern, may be to destroy a large part of their effectiveness. Only time, and continued study of the TM movement, will be able to supply an answer to this question.

Hare Krishna

One's first encounter with a group of Hare Krishna people is likely to be unforgettable. The men have their heads shaved except for a topknot or pony tail of long hair, and they wear dhotis (cloths wrapped around the waist and drawn up between the legs) and robes of burnt orange and pale yellow. The women wear their hair long and braided and dress in brightly colored saris. All wear a tilaka, the mark of Krishna—a daub of white clay or some other material that streaks down the forehead to a point between the eyes.

A group of them ranging in size from half a dozen to twenty might be found on the streets of any large city in America, from New York's Times Square to San Francisco's Ghiradelli Square. They begin thumping small drums, ringing bells and chanting "Hare Krishna." As the chanting goes on, the performers seem to be transported into a state of rapture. They begin clapping rhythmically and dancing about. The volume of chanting and clapping rises, and the dancing becomes more energetic, not wild or frenzied, but quite active. It is a sight strange enough to turn the head of even the most hardened city dweller, who is sure he has seen everything, and is surprised by nothing.

The first thought one gets is that this is a group of visiting monks from India, or some other equally distant and and exotic land. A closer inspection shows that the faces of these performers are distinctly American. Even the accents in which they chant "Hare Krishna, Hare Krishna" are American.

The Hare Krishna sect is probably the most picturesque and Eastern-looking of all the Eastern religions currently popular in the U.S. The sect believes, among other things, that merely chanting the holy name of God, or Krishna, will have an uplifting effect upon both he who does the chanting and any passer-by.

All Hindu religions are based on the ancient Vedic scriptures. There really is no single unified Hindu religion any more than there is a single unified Christian religion. Christianity is an umbrella under which one can place everything from Unitarians, who may not believe in God at all, to cults of snake handlers, who think that when they are filled with the Spirit they will be protected from the snake's venom. The Vedas are older than the Bible, and the religious groups that have grown up about them are even more varied and complex than those that have grown around the Bible. Hindu groups in which chanting is a central element go back to at least the fifteenth century, and are perhaps a great deal older.

The Hare Krishna people even hesitate to describe themselves as a religion. Rather, they say they are a cultural movement, which involves not only beliefs but an entire style of life. Hare Krishna people, like the adherents of many Eastern religions, do not hold that faith alone counts for a great deal. In order to find the inner peace and happiness that comes from knowing God, one must have a system for knowing God. The Hare Krishna people say they possess this system, and in the words of an offical publication of the group it is "Based on the scientific principles of spiritual understanding found in the Vedas, the oldest scriptures in the world. . . ."

Krishna, they say, is the Supreme Lord of the Universe. Man's spirit but not his body is part of Krishna. If one is entirely and scientifically dedicated to Krishna, then one may attain, in this lifetime, a state of "pure, eternal bliss, free from all anxiety." This state is the goal of the Hare Krishna people.

The Hare Krishna movement, or Krishna Consciousness, was brought to the United States in 1965 by A. C. Bhaktivedenta Swami Prabhupada. Prabhupada, as his devotees usually call him, was following advice given him some thirty years earlier by his own spiritual adviser. So it was that at the age of seventy Prabhupada, having renounced the world, boarded the merchant ship *Jaladuta* from Calcutta and landed at Boston Harbor. In India he had been a reasonably well-off man, but because of currency restrictions he was able to bring only seven dollars with him. In addition to that he had a suitcase full of Vedic scriptures that he had translated, and a letter of introduction to an Indian family in Pennsylvania.

Prabhupada went to New York City, where he stayed first with a Yoga society, then in a Bowery loft, and later in an apartment on West 72nd Street. Other yogis advised him to westernize his appearance and message. Prabhupada rejected the advice and went

Chanting dancing members of the Hare Krishna sect are familiar figures on the streets of many large American cities.

his own way. This elderly Indian with the strange outfit managed to pick up a few disciples from among young spiritual seekers in New York City. The disciples rented a storefront from him on the Lower East Side, or East Village, and the curious as well as the serious began to attend Prabhupada's nightly classes.

Most of the converts to Krishna Consciousness have come from among the dropouts from straight society. Of such young people Prabhupada has said, "That is their credit, they have rejected materialism but because of a poor fund of knowledge they have taken to drugs and animalistic sex life."

At the storefront Prabhupada served his disciples vegetarian meals and led them in chanting the Hare Krishna mantra, "Hare Krishna, Hare Krishna, Krishna, Krishna, Hare, Hare, Hare Rama, Hare Rama, Rama, Rama, Hare, Hare," to startled strollers in Tompkins Square Park.

The appeal of the early Hare Krishna movement was clearly aimed at the dropouts and drug users of the counterculture. One early flyer began with, "STAY HIGH FOREVER. No more Coming Down, Practice Krishna Consciousness. . . . END ALL BRINGDOWNS! TURN-ON through music, dance, philosophy, science, religion, and prasadam [spiritual food]."

In 1974 the Hare Krishna movement, or to give its proper name, the International Society for Krishna Consciousness (ISKCON), had some seventy branches throughout the United States, Europe and Asia. There are temples and ashrams in most of the country's larger cities, and ISKCON has even established its own school in Dallas, Texas. Presently the school has an enrollment of about 75. In addition, ISKCON runs various social service projects both in the United States and elsewhere, including India.

The group has even established a thriving business, Spiritual Sky Scented Products Company, which manufactures and distributes a significant percentage of the incense and other scented products sold in the U.S. Along with public contributions and the sale of its very attractive literature, ISKCON appears to be one of the most financially secure of all the unorthodox religions in America today.

When one enounters a Hare Krishna devotee on the street, he is likely to be handed a copy of the movement's magazine *Back to Godhead* and a flower or a stick of incense. There is no charge for any of this, but anyone who takes the material is requested and expected to contribute. This style of street soliciting is quite typical of unorthodox religious movements of all types.

In addition to their Indian dress, the Hare Krishnas put out a magazine that looks Indian, at least to Western eyes. While most unorthodox religions have tried to emulate the style of the underground press, ISKCON's publications have long stories about ancient Indian princes who became "pure devotees." The drawings, which are skillfully done, illustrate these stories in what I take to be a traditional Indian style. In any event there are no comic strips, no breezy new journalism style to attract the young. If you want Krishna Consiousness, you have to take it on its own terms.

For all its success, however, the Hare Krishna movement isn't really very large in total numbers. Thousands may attend a public Hare Krishna festival but there are only about 1,500 full-time disciples in the United States and another 1,500 worldwide. Because of the high visibility of its members, the group seems much larger.

When reporters asked Prabhupada about the small number of Krishna devotees he had gained in his six years in the West, he replied, "If you sell diamonds you cannot expect to have many customers. But a diamond is a diamond even if there are no customers."

According to ISKCON, it is really very easy to become a part of the Krishna Consciousness movement. "There is no need to convert from one religion to another. Krishna Consciousness is already within every one; it is spiritually natural for every living being. It must simply be awakened." The best way to awaken this consciousness is to joyfully chant the name of Krishna. If this chanting gives an individual real inner peace and a sense of brotherhood will all men, then one is partaking of Krishna Consciousness. You can join one of the street groups and chant and dance along with them.

But to become a true devotee is not so easy. It requires a drastic alteration in lifestyle. The most obvious thing one must do is adopt Indian dress. "Simple dress of the Vedic tradition," ISKCON calls it.

> The shaved head and mark of tilaka on the forehead (two straight lines made from white clay) have spiritual significance. Shaving one's head is a sign of detachment from the material pleasure, and a desire for spiritual development. Tilaka signifies that the body is a temple of God and must be used constantly in His service. The devotee's uniform also serves to remind others of both the need and the opportunity to receive spiritual guidance from a devotee.

It has also been suggested that the topknot or pigtail is worn so that the "Lord Krishna can pull one into greater consciousness."

The dress of the women has much less spiritual significance, and in fact, women hold a distinctly inferior position within Hare Krishna. Leaders of the movement say that women are naturally inclined to child rearing. Perhaps for this reason ISKCON has proved considerably less attractive to women than men. Men outnumber women in Hare Krishna by about three to one. One devotee was quoted as saying, "Men are more intelligent than women. Women give one a lot of nonsense."

Life in the society's ashrams is rigorous to the point of asceticism. Typically, devotees rise and bathe at 3:30 A.M. There are several hours of meditation and chanting until breakfast at 7:45, then classes and clean-up until the work day begins at 9:15. Devotees may work on ISKCON's many publishing projects or in the production and packaging of incense. But the primary work is bringing Krishna Consciousness to the world. They may go out chanting and passing out literature on the streets, or into schools and homes, wherever they are allowed to go. Lights out in the ashrams is 10:00 P.M.

The Krishna devotees strive for lives of "purity," and this means no "illicit sex." Marriages are allowed, but all sexual contact including kissing, even between married partners, is considered illicit

Hare Krishna leader Prahupada meets his followers during a stopover at New York's Kennedy Airport.

unless it is performed once a month at the optimum time for pro-creation. Even then each partner must engage in several hours of chanting beforehand, in order to cleanse the mind. Marriages are arranged by higher ranking members of the sect.

Meals are strictly vegetarian, and a portion is always offered to God before consumption. There is a prohibition not only on drugs and alcohol, but on all forms of stimulants such as tea and coffee.

There is also a prohibition on gambling, and this is extended to all forms of "mental speculation." Thus, devotees are not allowed to hold opinions other than those acceptable to Prabhupada and are, in fact, discouraged from thinking at all.

ISKCON is quite frank about the degree of mental and physical control it retains over its members. The *New York Times* quoted one devotee, Prajapati Das, the Krishna Consciousness name of a former social worker from Dallas, Texas: "The rigidity of behavior and thought control has a purpose. The regulations control activity. The control of activity reduces tensions, freeing the senses. The heightening of the senses enlarges the mind, and leads to a greater consciousness."

As with other Eastern religions that have become popular in the U.S., the mind—that is, any form of rational thought, any questioning of the basic precepts upon which the religion is based—is treated with unrelenting hostility. Mind is something to be suppressed or if possible trained out of individuals at a very early age.

New York Times reporter Eleanor Blau visited the Hare Krishna boarding school near Dallas, Texas. It is here that many children of cult members are sent to school. She observed this scene:

> Krishna Kumari was telling her kindergarten pupils a story about Lord Krishna and a bee the other day when she stopped to scold a boy for inattention.
>
> "Oh there's Jason listening to his mind, his garbage-pail mind," Krishna Kumari said. Jason put his hands to his eyes in shame. He stayed that way a long time, face tilted down, the topknot of hair sprouting from his otherwise shaved head.
>
> "Servant of the mind," the young teacher intoned, gazin at him. Then she resumed the tale."

Chanting and dancing are effective and widely used methods of banishing unpleasant thoughts and giving a troubled individual the feeling of being in touch with the infinite. Repetitive prayers like Hail Marys have long been used by Catholics, and religious mystics from Moslem dervishes to Hassidic Jews have been carried into transports of religious rapture by dancing. So for all their oddity of appearance and action there is nothing entirely unique or even uniquely Eastern about the basic practices of the Hare Krishna sect.

Repetitive chanting itself can produce some rather striking results which may have nothing whatever to do with the holiness of the name of Lord Krishna. In his book *Cults of Unreason,* British psychologist Christopher Evans comments on the strange effects of chanting:

> In fact psychologists know that when a word or brief phrase is repeated over and over again, it begins to change its characteristics in a peculiar way. This is not merely a matter of tongue-twisting (Hare Krishna soon becomes pretty muddled on repetition) for a word played repeatedly on a tape recorder will soon distort perceptually in the most strange way. The word kettle, for example, will soon be heard as petal, castle, rattle, etc. The phenomenon, which is an exceedingly striking one and which anyone can demonstrate to himself with a tape recorder and an endless loop of tape, has been the subject of much serious psychological experimentation and is believed to say something about the nature of the auditory recognition process. It is very likely that this odd effect is behind the evolution of the mantra, a phrase or prayer which repeated over and over again is supposed to acquire a special kind of spiritual significance. . . .

The extreme rigidity in thought and action required by the sect, and its unquestioning acceptance of Prabhupada as absolute leader, has led some unfriendly observers to speculate that the sect is nothing more than an exotic religious racket. Lester Kinsolving, who writes a syndicated column on religion, compared Prabhupada with Krishna Venta, a notorious religious racketeer of the 1950s. But most observers conclude that even if they do not care for Hare Krishna, both its members and its leader are sincere in their beliefs.

One can not be entirely certain whether Prabhupada is regarded, or regards himself, as divine. He certainly never says that he is, but he has also written, "An incarnation of the supreme Lord never declares Himself to be an incarnation. But His followers, with reference to the context of the authoritative Scriptures, must ascertain who is an incarnation and who is a pretender." Hare Krishna devotees certainly do not think of Prabhupada as a pretender, but he is also not the center of a personality cult as is the Guru Maharaj Ji.

For a group that discourages thought, devotees often stress the "intelligence" of their converts. "This is a movement of intelligent men," one told a *New York Times* reporter. "We have plenty of educated men who have been searching for God for years and discovered Him in Krishna. They have to be intelligent to reach a point when they ask 'Why?' They see order in the universe and realize where there is order there is meaning."

Hare Krishna philosophy contains the traditional rejection of the material world, which brings only suffering and death. "We are not these bodies—that is the first basic lesson of Krishna Consciousness. We understand that we have an eternal relationship with God and once that is developed then peace and prosperity follows."

While many parents are horrified when their children join the sect, at least a small percentage are deeply relieved. Parents of the Hare Krishna people do not see their children often, but one of the first rules of the sect is reconciliation with parents. There is nothing like the hostility to parents preached by the Children of God. Young people who had been on drugs or in trouble with the law are at least out of harm's way in the ascetic life of the ashram.

Most sects do not like to talk about dropouts, for dropouts imply that there is something less than perfect in the sect's teachings, though of course there are many ways to explain or rationalize those who fall away. There are no hard figures on the number of Hare Krishna dropouts. There have been estimates that some 30 per cent drop out within the first year, but after that the dropout rate is a modest 10 per cent. The movement is, however, a mere six years old, and no one can predict what will happen to it after the death of Prabhupada.

Perhaps it is a Western prejudice, but most of us tend to regard Eastern religions as rather passive in seeking out new converts. One frequently hears Americans who are interested in Eastern religions say that the true gurus do not look for disciples, but wait for the disciples to find them. Another common belief, or perhaps just another misapprehension, is that Eastern religions are very tolerant of one another, preaching that there are many roads to truth and that it matters little which road the devout seeker wishes to follow.

But the Hare Krishna people are aggressive in making themselves known. By their unique dress and loud public chanting they quite literally force themselves on the attention of the passer-by. Hare Krishna chanters are often chased away or arrested by the police who claim that their chanting is a public nuisance. This harassment rarely succeeds, for the Hare Krishnas are back the next day at the very same spot to take up the chant. A lot of people react with real anger toward the Hare Krishnas, perhaps because their chanting really is disturbing, but more likely because they are such a strange-looking group that their very appearance releases hostility. I talked to a number of people who lived in the vicinity of a large Hare Krishna center in Brooklyn, N.Y. None of them liked the Hare Krishnas, though they were not individuals who could normally be classed as bigoted or narrow-minded. No one seemed to know exactly why he disliked the Hare Krishnas, either. No other unorthodox religious group seems to arouse quite so much unreasoned anger from its neighbors.

For their part, the Hare Krishnas are ready to dispute religion with anyone and everyone. They often have conducted heated arguments with Jesus People who are contending for possession of the same popular street corner. Hare Krishnas descended on the Guru Maharaj Ji's Millennium '73 in force and took on premies and Jesus People alike, in one of the more colorful religious confrontations of recent years.

Prabhupada has written scornfully of other systems of Yoga, ". . . the bogus yoga system which is going on in the West these days. The yoga systems which have been introduced into the West by so-called yogis are not *bona fide*."

Some of his disciples put the matter even more bluntly. Hrdayananda dasa Gosvami, speaking at the University of Florida, said:

> If we accept the arguments of so-called yogis that no matter what we do we will all merge into the same point, there is no question of free will because we would all be compelled to come together, although we are acting and desiring differently. And without free will, what is the use of liberation? Liberation is meaningless without free will. Therefore the Supreme Lord Krsna [Krishna] advises us

to surrender freely to Him. But if we are stubborn like
asses and want to worship someone other than Krsna we
will get an inferior result.

Hrdayananda dasa Gosvami also had little use for allowing
schools to teach religion other than that of Hare Krishna: "To
understand God, one needs intelligent discrimination. But people
do not understand this. For example, the schools say, 'If we allow
you to teach Krsna [Krishna] consciousness, then we must allow
everyone to come and teach his idea.' But that is such foolishness!
. . . Discrimination based on ignorance is useless, but discrimination based on quality is necessary."

It is this intolerant, undemocratic, even rather petulant quality
that is the least attractive side of Hare Krishna to this outsider. Yet
to the movement's devotees these qualities are absolutely necessary. They have made a great and very difficult commitment that
has wrenched them completely out of the mainstream of Western
life, and made them objects of ridicule and hatred. They must feel
that they, and they alone, are in possession of the truth, and that
the rest of the world is made up of fools.

We have no right to judge the Hare Krishna people harshly for
their attitude of exclusivity. It is common to all small religious
groups, particularly those who dare to be openly and obviously
different. They do, in fact, face real discrimination, ridicule and
misunderstanding because they refuse to conform to Western
standards of appearance and behavior.

It is instructive to remind ourselves that according to the Bible
Jesus told his own followers, "If ye were of the world, the world
would love his own: but because ye are not of the world, but I
have chosen you out of the world, therefore the world hateth you"
[John 15:19].

Subud

No one from Subud is going to stop you on the street and ask you to attend a meeting or force a piece of literature on you. Subud does not proselytize. It also does not seek, or particularly appreciate, publicity, and it will not allow you to take pictures of its ceremonies. When I called Subud's New York office, they were not inclined to be cooperative; indeed, they sounded quite suspicious.

But it isn't that Subud is a secret society, or feels it has anything to hide. The attitude of the group stems primarily from the belief that Subud can't really be described anyway, and that most of what is said about it is going to be misleading at best.

And in truth, Subud has in the past received some unwelcome publicity, particularly back in the late 1950s when it was first introduced in England. An early enthusiast for Subud was actress Eva Bartok. The presence of this celebrity at Subud headquarters in London brought out a flock of reporters, and a fair number of miracle seekers. Since that time Subud has worked hard at maintaining a low profile. It is obviously not easy for an outsider (or apparently even an insider) to write about Subud.

A brochure printed by Subud defines the name as "an abbreviation of three Sanskrit words—*Susila, Budhi,* and *Dharma. Susila* means: right living in accordance with the Will of God. *Budhi* means: the divine force within every creature including man. *Dharma* means: the attitude of trust, sincerity, and submission toward Almighty God."

That defines the word without really explaining it. The brochure continues, "Subud is neither a teaching nor a philosophy. It does not add anything new to what has already been revealed to mankind through the great religions, but it does lead the individual, gradually, to a deeper understanding of the meaning and place of religion in man's life."

A bit further on the brochure informs us:

> Subud is neither a sect nor a substitute for conventional religion. It has not separated itself from any church and is not opposed to any denomination. . . . Subud does not take official positions in matters of politics or philosophy. Members are absolutely free in these regards to make up their own minds. Subud likewise has no desire, through worldly influence or power, to change or improve the world. Finally, Subud should not be considered some kind of quick-and-easy cure-all for the ills of our times.

That is a good deal about what Subud isn't—but what is it? Subud is most frequently described as "an experience." Members of local Subud groups meet together usually twice a week for something called Latihan, an Indonesian word for exercise. It isn't really an exercise, though at times the Latihans can become quite physically inclined. "It is," says the Subud brochure, "a way of worshiping God which is received from within." During Latihan the Subud member is somehow put in touch with "higher energies."

The gatherings at which Latihan takes place are open only to

Subud members, and they are extremely reluctant to discuss what goes on at those regular gatherings. As a result, Latihan may seem very mysterious, even perhaps a bit sinister. But Subud members insist that they are not trying to create mystification. They say that they do not try to describe Laihan because it is a highly individualized experience and, therefore, indescribable. But if Subud and its central experience, Latihan, cannot be described from the inside, we can at least trace the development of the movement, and see what it looks like from the outside.

Subud began with Muhammad Subuh, or *Bapak*, as he is now called. Bapak is an Indonesian term of respect for an elderly man, roughly "father." Subud is not greatly interested in giving the details of Bapak's life. He was born in Java in 1901, into an Islamic family. As a young man he pursued a spiritual quest, visiting teachers both within and outside of Islamic tradition. Feeling nothing would come of it, he abandoned the search and became a bookkeeper and minor government official, married and began to raise a family.

In 1925 something happened to Bapak. For the next three years, according to his followers, he found himself spontaneously in the process of the Latihan, roughly, being in contact with God or "higher energies." He was puzzled by this and even tried to avoid the experience, but to no avail. A few years later Bapak received a revelation. He had been chosen as the means by which this inner contact with the Power of God could be transmitted to others. I will not attempt to describe either the contact or the transmission, but it is not something that can be accomplished by an individual unaided.

Says the Subud literature:

> Some members, specially authorized by Pak Subuh, assist in the transmission of the Subud contact. When one of these "helpers" follows his own Latihan in the presence of an applicant, the contact is transmitted, and the inner receiving begins automatically in the new member. It is necessary to receive the contact in this way to be able to participate in the Latihan.

The movement spread in the East, particularly in Bapak's native Indonesia, for about a quarter century, but didn't reach the West until 1957. At that time a group of Englishmen who had been interested in religion and mysticism heard of Bapak and invited him to England. He accepted.

To anyone expecting some sort of overpowering Messiah figure, or dramatically ascetic holy man, Bapak must have been a big disappointment. He turned out to be a slight, soft-spoken man who wore glasses, went to the movies, smoked and was extremely modest about his accomplishments. He was in fact a very ordinary man who in the eyes of his followers had contact with a very extraordinary power.

After its initial burst of not altogether welcome publicity, Subud has settled down and spread quietly through America and Europe. It is said to be established in at least seventy countries, and that there are some sixty Subud centers in the U.S., with somewhere around 2,000 individuals in regular attendance. The various groups nationally and internationally are loosely linked together, but there is no real hierarchy except for the existence of Bapak's personally chosen "helpers" who oversee various centers in their areas. Bapak himself occasionally makes world tours, to visit the various centers.

In the West at least, Subud members are generally middle class, though they have come from a wide variety of backgrounds. No one in Subud is required to quit his job, become celibate, or give up eating meat. One can even continue to attend whatever church he likes.

But changes can come about. "It may happen, to be sure, that after a time a particular member may deem it right to change his profession, move to another place, or even change his first name. This, however, is an entirely personal matter, subject to the decision of the individual." An individual's daily life may improve as a result of the new "inner freedom" gained through Subud, but this is not the chief goal of Subud.

Anyone over the age of eighteen may receive Latihan, though in places where the legal age is twenty-one parental approval must be obtained. After applying, there is a waiting period of about three months, during which the candidates are interviewed and advised to read more about Subud and ask any questions they might have. They are also allowed, if they wish, to sit outside of the room in which Latihan is taking place.

What they may hear is described by Jacob Needleman in his book *The New Religions* (a book recommended to me by the New York Subud Center):

> At first it may be a soft murmuring; or perhaps a single loud shout. From the women's room (latihans are segregated by sex) he may hear the beginnings of soft sirenesque moaning. Then, any or all of the following: animal sounds, groans, perhaps fierce and strident shrieks. Or chanting and beautiful wordless singing accompanied by a deep ground bass ever louder or softer. Soon body sounds are added. Thumpings, running sounds. The din rises or in an instant subsides, only to rise again deeper and more clamorous than ever. At full blast, the latihan may sound like nothing so much as jungle animals, or maniacal, savage rites, or an eerie convocation of demons and banshees. At other times it seems a deeply religious choir, or a joyous raucous celebration, a Corybantic frenzy, or a madhouse. It is, in a sense, all of these, yet none of them. There may be sudden breathtaking harmonies; a sweet fragment of melody; or deepthroated sobbing.

Yet when the half hour is over, those leaving the Latihan hall do not look like individuals who had just engaged in a mad frenzied rite. They are not flushed, exhausted or wild-eyed. They look like a group of people, says Needleman, who had just left a quiet lecture.

Inside the Latihan hall there may indeed be a good deal of screaming and jumping around, but this is not really what is happening say those aquainted with the experience. The true Latihan takes place within an individual. But it is not nearly so easy to describe what is happening within a person. Says the Subud brochure:

"During the Latihan, the mind, the heart, the will, and the desires are each rendered more or less inactive. . . ." In such a state of submission, the individual is "open" to higher forces which guide one through a process of purification, and yet one is both fully conscious and in control at all times of whether one wishes to continue or not. ·

According to a Subud spokesman, "Generally speaking Latihans have become more quiet over the years. The process of purification usually starts in the physical (which is why there may be noise and/or leaping around) and then continues through the various aspects of emotional, mental, and other human attributes."

What makes Latihan virtually impossible to describe is that everyone experiences it differently, and that the experience itself is constantly changing.

Not everyone finds the experience of Latihan a rewarding one. At the Latihan a person is advised to try to stand in a relaxed way. Some people just stand around, often for months, waiting for something to happen. Either something finally does, or they leave discouraged. Others experience a genuine crisis. Says Needleman, "In short, some people do seem to 'go crazy' in Subud." It is the task of the helpers in the Latihan to bring them out of it.

One of the earliest British supporters of Subud received a cracked rib from an individual who went careening violently around the room before he could be subdued. There have been charges that Subud has affected some individuals very strangely indeed. One man is said to have died mysteriously shortly after the experience. On the other hand there have been stories of miraculous cures that have taken place as the result of the Latihan.

Bapak has strongly warned Subud followers against trying Latihan too often; twice a week is recommended, three times a week tops, because the process of purification can become too intense and cause a crisis. He also warns against any attempt to force or hurry the experience, for the same reason.

In the end one wonders if there is any fundamental difference between the experience of Subud and the experiences undergone by devotees of a variety of other religions. Is a person in Latihan really any different from an individual overcome by the Holy Spirit at a revival meeting? They, too, often jump, run around and make strange noises, and, incidentally, such activities are referred to as "exercises." Is the person who has received Knowledge at the hands of one of the Guru Maharaj Ji's mahatmas more or less in contact with the higher energies than an individual who has been "opened" with the aid of one of Babak's helpers?

Such questions are really unanswerable to an outsider. But in terms of what can be seen or described, the experiences seem very similar indeed.

The
Occult

Witchcraft

A southern California preacher by the name of Hershel Smith has attracted a great deal of attention traveling around the country in a van loaded with tarot cards, horoscopes, black candles, skulls, robes and a lot of other paraphernalia associated with the occult. His van has been dubbed "the Witchmobile." Smith warns his mostly young audiences against following strange and diabolical doctrines and sects. Under the heading of devil worship Smith includes followers of Eastern religions like Hare Krishna. Witchcraft, of course, is a special target.

Hershel Smith's appeal is crude, but he isn't the only man in America today denouncing witchcraft. Witchcraft and the occult are among the most frequent targets of the Jesus People, and they are particularly proud when they are able to convert someone from such "diabolical ideas." Smith himself claims to have been a "Satanist" before returning to the Assemblies of God, the church of his youth. The biblical injunction, "Thou shalt not suffer a witch to live," is often heard as part of denunciations from Jesus People.

Fundamentalist preachers from Billy Graham on down have become increasingly strident in their warnings against the popularity of witchcraft and the occult. Indeed, a popular occult publication recently labeled Billy Graham as the potential Grand Inquisitor of a new outbreak of witch burnings.

At their 1974 convention, the Daughters of the American Revolution passed a resolution condemning the teaching of courses in witchcraft and magic, though there is enormous student interest in such subjects.

Yet most of those who denounce witchcraft display a shocking ignorance of what it was, or is.

Modern witchcraft has a severe image problem. To many, like Hershel Smith, the word "witch" immediately conjures up sinister images of black masses and infant sacrifices. A more sophisticated though unreligious view holds that modern witchcraft is the creation of a handful of eccentric exhibitionists who like to dress in funny outfits and get on television by saying outrageous things.

Both views are misleading. In fact, there are thousands of perfectly "straight" witches in America today. Most of them practice quietly, even secretly. These are jokingly referred to as "closet witches." Your next door neighbor may be one, but that is nothing to be alarmed about. Modern witchcraft is a religion, and classed as such by the Internal Revenue Service. Modern witches also insist that the words "witch" and "witchcraft" be capitalized. But these words have been used so loosely that I will capitalize them only when referring to specific groups.

Witches feel that because of Judeo-Christian stereotypes they have been seriously misunderstood and hideously treated through history. They point to the uncounted tens and perhaps hundreds of thousands who were tortured, burned and hanged during the appalling persecutions of witchcraft during the Middle Ages. America, they remind us, has the infamous distinction of being the site of the Western world's last major witchcraft trials, those that took place in Salem, Massachusetts, in 1692 and resulted in the death by hanging of nineteen accused witches.

While witches are no longer being hanged in America, they are occasionally being discriminated against. Early in 1974 Robert J. Williams, a psychologist at the Kansas State Industrial Reformatory, was fired when a local paper revealed the fact that he was an initiated Witch. Williams had been practicing witchcraft quietly for some time, and it was the publicity, rather than the witchcraft itself, that landed him in trouble. Williams appealed to the State Civil Service Commission to get his job back, and he won. Others have not been so fortunate.

When Willams was asked why witches were so secretive, he replied, "History speaks for itself."

Dr. Leo Louis Martello, who says that he is both a hereditary and an initiated Witch, is one of the leading witchcraft figures on the East Coast. He is not only a public Witch, he is an aggressive one. His interest in improving the lot of his co-religionists in modern society is reflected in the fact that he founded the Witches Liberation Movement, and is director of the Witches Anti-Defamation League. In 1970 Dr. Martello hit the newspapers when a Witchcraft group was denied a permit to hold a ritual celebration in Central Park on Halloween. He contacted the New York Civil Liberties Union, which arranged for the permit. The ceremony itself was quite a tame affair. Central Park had been the site of far stranger activities.

Now this might provoke a smile, but the smile would be misplaced. Leo Louis Martello is not joking around. He is a serious and very often angry man. He feels that witchcraft has been so badly maligned in the past, and that he personally has so often been misquoted, that he no longer grants interviews. He even had his phone disconnected. But he did agree to answer a series of written questions which provide a good starting point for a look at this most misunderstood of unorthodox religions.

Q. I take it that witchcraft is an ancient pagan religion. What are its basic beliefs?

A. We believe in Reincarnation, in the Law of Karma, "as ye sow so shall ye reap." Or as the Witch tenet goes: "An ye harm none do what ye will. Do good and it will return threefold. Do evil and it will return threefold." We worship and identify with the

Horned God, Lord of the Hunt and the Underworld, and the
Mother Goddess, especially the latter (Mother Earth, Mother Nature). Without the female principle (women) man wouldn't be
here. We believe that our deities need our help as much as we need
theirs. Our dieties and our faith is a pagan, pre-Christian religion.
. . . Unlike other religions every person accepted into a coven becomes a priest or priestess and takes an active part in the ceremonies. For this reason we have no laity as yet. Large congrega-
tions made up of passive observers, rather than active religionists,
is foreign to our make-up.

Q. Is modern witchcraft a direct and unbroken survival from
pre-Christian times, or is it a rediscovery of old beliefs?

A. Today it's mostly a rediscovery of "fragments of a forgotten
faith." During Inquisitional times covens became scattered, had no
contact with one another in order to prevent discovery and be-
trayal. Since most of Witchcraft was an oral tradition much was
lost. However, in certain continental covens, especially the Sicilian
branch, there is an unbroken line that goes back thousands of
years. My ancestors come from the town of Castrogiovanni, the
ancient Enna, which was the seat of worship to the Goddess Demeter and her daughter Persephone (Roman Ceres and Proser-
pina). The Greek Goddesses supplanted the Sikelian Goddess who
had similar attributes. We still use the secret name of Sikelian
deities. In Italy and Sicily *la vecchia religione* was an underground
spring that has only recently erupted to the surface.

Q. Explain the differences between witchcraft and Satanism.

A. Witchcraft is a pre-Christian faith worshipping the Pagan
deities. Satanism is reverse or perverse Christianity. Witches don't
believe in the devil, heaven, hell or limbo. It [witchcraft] tends to be
matriarchial whereas both Christianity and Satanism are patriarchal
and male chauvinist. The latter two are merely opposite sides of the
same coin. Witchcraft, as the Old Religion, is a coin of a different
vintage, predating both. Satanism is the dark side of Christianity,
as were the book and the movies of "Rosemary's Baby" and "The
Exorcist." So-called "Black Masses" are performed by renegade
Christians who wish to pervert and blaspheme their own beliefs.
Witches don't perform "masses" whether "Black" or "White." True

Witchcraft is a nature-oriented earth religion. Theologically, Witches are non-Christian, whereas Satanists are anti-Christian.

Q. Do you have any idea how many practicing witches there are in the United States today?

A. No one knows for sure since most covens are still secret. The secrecy is because (1) the Craft [one of the many names applied to witchcraft] itself is a Mystery Religion; (2) most practitioners want to worship quietly and not be bothered either by inquisitive reporters or prejudicially misinformed neighbors; and (3) for their families' sake they can't afford to jeopardize their jobs because "Witchcraft" is still linked with devil worship and evil due to centuries of brainwashing by the Church and a sensationalist press. However, Witchcraft covens are closely related to the upsurge of Pagan groups through the country and they exist in every major city and in every state. There are thousands of Witches and Pagans and this is growing every day. . . .

Q. How are Witchcraft groups organized? By that I mean what is the structure of the individual group and is there any national or international Witchcraft organization?

A. Every coven is autonomous, with 13 members the maximum. When a coven becomes oversubscribed one of the priestesses branches off, if qualified to form her own. . . . At the Grand Sabbat many of the covens join together for festivities. There are some groups who have incorporated themselves as churches or religious bodies. The Witches International Craft Associates (WICA), the Witches Anti-Defamation League, and the Witches Liberation Movement are interrelated groups and international. Each group is run by a High Priestess and a High Priest (who symbolically represent the Goddess and her consort the Horned God on earth) and they go by the rules in their secret *Book of Shadows,* a sort of Witches' Bible.

Q. How does one become a Witch?

A. There are basically two kinds of Witches: Hereditary and Initiated. The former are born into Witch families and taught. However, there is no such thing as automatic Witch knowledge. This must be learned. Initiated witches have been accepted into a coven after a long trial period. "Many are called but few are chosen."

The reason is that most people who seek initiation into a coven are wrongly motivated by either Judeo-Christian misconceptions, false ideas of sexual orgies or drugs, or phantasies of having "power" over others. [In an earlier letter Dr. Martello noted that no genuine Witch coven will admit anyone under the age of eighteen without parental consent. In some states the minimum age is twenty-one.]

Q. Witchcraft has long been associated in the popular mind with magic. Do Witches possess or can they develop any powers that we might call magical, supernatural, paranormal or psychic? Give a few examples.

A. Magick [*sic*—this spelling is popular with several occult groups] is an integral part of true Witchcraft. But the powers of a Witch are not separated from his or her faith; they emanate from it. That's why many people who are only interested in the "power" aspect of Witchcraft are disappointed. They have neither the training, nor the philosophy, nor the theology to make it work. . . . For years we've had a Healing Registry in which anyone who is troubled or ill can request that his or her name is placed on it. These names are read off and concentrated upon when Witches dance in order to raise the Cone of Power. There is no charge for this service. We promise nothing except to do what we say we will. Others have reported fantastic results after they've exhausted all other possible means. . . . All of this could be considered a belief in "magick."

Q. I know that witches have often been slandered as practitioners of black or evil magic. Do witches hold to the Christian idea of loving one's enemies or will witches turn their power against their enemies?

A. Every Witch, as well as every person, has the right to self-defense. But no one has the right to initiate force against another. Some Witchcraft traditions seem to have a "Christian" view of karma: that if one hits back, even in self-defense, there will be reprisals. My own tradition doesn't accept this concept. We give no one the right to do us wrong. Nor do we buy the concept of *unearned* love: To love one's enemies as well as one's friends totally devalues that emotion, and says that in terms of your own feelings your friends are no better than your enemies.

Dr. Leo Louis Martello

Q. Witches are supposed to hold their meetings in the nude. Do they, are if so, why?

A. Some do and some don't. Depends on their tradition. I've worked with both robed and skyclad [nude] traditions. The reason for nudity is that these Witches believe that clothes interfere with the power that emanates from their bodies. Another is that amongst Witches there are no class distinctions. A third reason comes from the book *Aradia, or Gospel of the Witches* by C. G. Leland which says, "as the sign that ye are truly free, ye shall be naked in your rites." My own tradition is robed and we feel that true psychic power can penetrate steel walls so clothes are no obstacle. The question is usually asked by people who were reared in the Judeo-Christian idea of nudity being "immodest" and worse. Witches generally have a healthy view toward the body: What's one nude body more or less?

Q. There appears to be a good deal of commercialization in witchcraft. Would you care to comment on this?

A. I wonder if you were interviewing a Catholic priest or Christian minister, if you would say, "There appears to be a good deal of commercialization in Christianity," especially in view of the fact that they own billions of dollars in tax-free property. . . . Another point: There may be a karmic reason for this supposed commercialization. During Inquisitional times Witches, Pagans, Jews and those called Heretics had all of their properties confiscated by the Church. When have any of their descendants been compensated by reparations? Witch priests and priestesses are not paid a salary, they do not pass a collection plate, they do not own thousands of tax-free churches, and the majority of them don't even take advantage of the traveling discount rates offered to other clergymen.

Q. What future do you see for Witchcraft?

A. Withcraft, as the Old Religion, and other Pagan faiths will one day have magnificent temples to the Goddess. However, just as there are many differences amongst Christians (Catholics, Presbyterians, Baptists, Lutherans, Methodists, etc.) and Jews (Orthodox, Reform, Conservative) so too are there various traditions and differences amongst Witches. At present there is an attempt at working out these differences, more and more Witches are "going public" and getting legal Church charters, groups are forming all over the world, and there is an Ecumenical spirit that is bringing the different factions together.

Another well-known public Witch is Gavin Frost. Gavin, a Welshman by birth, is the teacher and most audible expositor of the Welsh traditionalist strain in American Witchcraft. "Wales has a particularly strong oral tradition of Witchcraft," he says. An ancient Welsh coven is still alive and well at Bettws-y-coed in Wales, he insists. Gavin and his wife Yvonne run the School and

Church of Wicca out of their farm in (appropriately enough) Salem, Missouri. I asked him whether being a self-announced Witch in America's heartland had created any difficulties. "Not at all," he replied. "My neighbors are farmers, and when they find out I'm a Witch they come and ask me when is the proper time to plant the corn."

Gavin is not as expansive about the ultimate future of witchcraft in the world, but he is much less alarmed over its present status. "I've heard a lot of rumors about the persecution of Witches today, but I haven't really seen much evidence to back up these rumors." He is unsure whether persecution is on the increase. How many witches are there in America today? Gavin's estimate, which he freely admits is entirely speculative, is between four and five hundred thousand.

As for the future, Gavin sees Witchcraft playing a small though important part in a future Pagan revival that will mark the Age of Aquarius. "People keep saying the Age of Aquarius is dawning now, but it isn't due for several hundred years yet." Witchcraft, he believes, will never become a mass movement because it takes too much intelligence to become a Witch.

John Ray, a follower of Gavin's Welsh tradition, is an announced Witch who works in the post office and lives in a middle-class New Jersey town. "I'm in my forties," says Ray. "Most of the people in my coven are over thirty-five. This is a serious thing, it isn't just a teen-age fling."

While Ray admits that he gets kidded a lot by his co-workers, he doesn't really mind. "I announced that I was a Witch because I wanted to show that a person could be different." He finds that, secretly, a lot of people are interested, and half believe in the power of witches. "One of the loudest skeptics came up to me privately, and asked if I could work some sort of a healing spell for his blind eye."

Witchcraft, the Old Religion, Wicca, the Craft; these are all terms that witches have used to describe their religion. Most witches, by the way, avoid the term warlock, saying only that there are male witches and female witches. But squabbles over terminology appear to be an inevitable part of the subject. A much more serious argument concerns the antiquity of witchcraft itself.

The term witchcraft is a broad one. We must emphasize that what we are discussing here has little directly to do with African witchcraft, Indian witchcraft or any other supposedly "primitive" form of witchcraft. In the sense we mean it, witchcraft is a European tradition, and while there are many similarities with witchcraft in other parts of the world, these may well be coincidental.

Most nonoccult historians doubt that there ever was any well-organized or coherent witch cult or religion in Europe during medieval times or any other time. There were, however, plenty of people who were trying to practice magic, an activity often frowned upon by the official church. There were also customs surviving from pagan times, particularly in remote areas. There were heretics with strange ideas, some of which were taken from Middle Eastern religions, and there were more out and out rebels against the rigid strictures of medieval Christianity than is commonly believed.

According to most scholars, all of these beliefs and movements were lumped together under the title of witchcraft. While this diversity of belief indicates that medieval Christianity was not as monolithic as it once appeared, it does not automatically mean that witchcraft existed as a large underground religion. Indeed, some contended that the whole idea of a witch cult was really the invention of bigoted and corrupt witch hunters who immediately labeled all unorthodox thought and practice as diabolical.

The theory that witchcraft was not a diabolical conspiracy, or an insane fantasy, but rather a large and powerful, but highly secretive pagan religion, was first brought to public attention in the 1920s by Margaret Murray, a British anthropologist. In general historians scoffed at her theories, and even her supporters were somewhat embarrassed by some of her wilder ideas. For example, she believed that Joan of Arc, as well as many of the kings and queens of England, were secret leaders of the witch cult. Still, her books on the subject of witchcraft became quite popular, though more among those interested in occultism than among scholars.

One of the legacies Professor Murray apparently bequeathed to modern witchcraft was the coven of thirteen. She said that evidence from medieval witchcraft trials indicated that witches were organized into groups or covens of thirteen. Other scholars reexamining the same evidence hold that there was no standard size for witchcraft groups, and that the evidence itself is highly suspect.

Margaret Murray was followed by the poet and scholar Robert Graves. He wrote a book called *The White Goddess* which held that mankind's original religion was worship of a Mother Goddess, and that this worship was ultimately driven underground by the rise of male-dominated Judeo-Christian tradition. This old religion surfaced, contended Graves, in witchcraft.

Perhaps the single most significant influence on the development of modern witchcraft was Gerald Gardner. Gardner, a former British customs official in Malaya and a man of wide-ranging, if rather bizarre, interests, wrote a book claiming that he was a practicing Witch and the member of an ancient coven that had carried on the traditions of the Old Religion for centuries.

According to Gardner, he has been contacted by a representative from this ancient group of British Witches shortly before the outbreak of World War II. The Witches agreed to initiate Gardner into the coven because of his interest in the occult and because of his own ancestors had also been Witches. A few years later, said Gardner, his superiors gave him permission to "go public." Gardner also claimed that his coven had kept Hitler from invading England during World War II by performing a powerful magical spell, and that earlier British Witches had used the same power successfully against Napoleon.

There is no independent evidence that Gardner ever was in contact with a witch coven, indeed no independent evidence that all his witchcraft stories were not complete fabrications. What we do know, however, is that Gardner as an enthusiastic occultist had many friends in the British occult world. A large number of his "ancient traditions" appear to be drawn more from nineteenth- and twentieth-century British occultism than from any ancient pagan religion. P. E. I. Bonewits, a rising young star in occultism, is rather blunt when he says that Gardner "worked taking material from any source that didn't run too fast to get away."

But lack of a consistent philosophy didn't bother Gardner, nor does it bother most modern Witches, and perhaps it shouldn't. As pagans they see many forces at work in the universe, and believe that knowledge and power may come from many sources. Those in the Judeo-Christian tradition, the Witches believe, suffer from a sort of tunnel vision, in which they see only one source for truth and power. Thus the charge that modern Witches are inconsistent really misses the point, for in the pagan view there is no need for consistency. In the past, pagans freely accepted one another's gods and rituals without being hypocritical. This tolerance, however, does not prevent modern witchcraft groups from squabbling over what may appear to the outsider to be minor points of doctrine.

Gerald Gardner managed to attract a good deal of notoriety, some money, and a group of disciples. He moved out to the Isle of Man and was reported to have briefly joined a Manx coven. He purchased the Witch's Mill and Kitchen Museum from a man named Cecil Williamson. After Gardner's death in 1964, the contents of his museum were sold and are now on display at the Fisherman's Wharf in San Francisco.

Like so much about modern witchcraft, it is a bit difficult to know when Gardner was serious and when he was putting us on. Gavin Frost said that Gardner had told him that the tales of being related to witches in ancient times, and how he was in touch with a tradition that had been handed down virtually without change for centuries, had been exaggerated for effect. Occultists have long speculated on just what sort of "ancient coven" Gardner might have been in contact with, but no one seems to know for sure.

Gardner may have borrowed a lot of other people's ideas, and exaggerated or simply made up many stories, but witchcraft as he explained it caught on. By the 1950s there was a whole parade of self-proclaimed "kings and queens of witches" who were appearing on television and radio and giving newspaper interviews. This was mostly show business, publicity for individuals who were supporting themselves with lecture fees, or by writing books on "real" witchcraft, or simply for people who liked to get on television and get their names into the newspapers. This type of publicity is one of the main reasons why it is difficult to take witchcraft seriously as a religion. But the witches say that they should not be judged only by the highly visible publicity seekers. While all of this hoopla was going on, they say, many people were forming small secret covens, in an attempt to rediscover and practice the ancient traditions of Witchcraft.

Currently there appears to be less stress on witchcraft as an ancient cult, and more recognition of it as a modern attempt to rediscover old traditions and rituals. Bonewits seriously questioned the existence of a witch cult at all, much less is survival into the present century. "Never at any time until the persecution of the mid-1400s to the mid-1700s were Witches considered by anyone (priest, magician, wizard or peasant) to be the representatives of an underground religious movement."

He went on to say, "I am not attacking the religious or mystical significance of the Witchcult. It brings much comfort and happiness to its members. I just wish that it would accept the fact that it is a 20th century reconstruction of elements from various prehistoric fertility religions, and stop trying to be something it is not."

Most witches would disagree with Bonewits' conclusions, yet he delivered these words at a Witchmeet, a major gathering of witches and other pagans held in St. Paul, Minnesota, in 1973, and he was not immediately hooted out of the room. The speech was later reprinted in its entirety in *Gnostica News,* one of the major publications covering the Witchcraft and Pagan movement. Most witches would certainly agree that a tradition need not be ancient or "pure" in order to be effective.

Dr. Martello, and particularly Gavin Frost, emphasized the rediscovery side of modern witchcraft. Gavin said that modern witchcraft was a very pragmatic religion, not bound by any set of rigid traditions, but willing to incorporate whatever traditions or rituals that seemed to work. John Ray almost appeared to regard witchcraft as merely a frame in which he could pursue "deeper" studies in mysticism.

Some of Gavin's own rhetoric is very like the mystical naturalism that has grown up on the fringes of the ecology movement. "We recognize that our intelligence gives us a unique responsibility toward our environment. We seek to live in harmony with Nature, in ecological balance offering fulfillment to life and consciousness within an evolutionary concept." This is obviously a very long way from the popular ideas of the deals with the Devil and black masses.

Witchcraft has also attracted the attention of some feminists. Many modern witches worship or revere the Goddess as at least the equal of the Horned God, and stress that the creative powers of the universe are both masculine and feminine. During the witchcraft persecutions many more women than men were put to death as witches, and today the popular image of the witch is still an old woman in black robe and peaked cap. Some feminists have tried to identify witchcraft as a feminist religion ruthlessly suppressed in a male-dominated society.

One of the early feminist organizations in the 1960s was called WITCH—Women's International Terrorist Corps from Hell. Carrying brooms and wearing black robes and peaked caps, the members of WITCH often appeared at women's rights demonstrations. WITCH was part put-on, part guerrilla theater and part serious. Even today feminist publications occasionally have articles describing witchcraft as the Old Religion. These articles appear to put more stock in the historical authenticity of a witch cult than do many practicing witches.

What fascinates most people, though, are the questions, "What do witches do?" and "What happens at the secret rites of witchcraft?" Well, of course, if the rites are truly secret no outsider can say what happens. Besides, as we have already stressed, Witchcraft is by no means a monolithic movement. Each coven, group, tradition or what have you is perfectly free to adapt or invent whatever rites it chooses, and most make use of that freedom, so one cannot generalize. But an example given by San Francisco Witch Aidan Kelly to reporters for *Time* magazine is as representative as any. Kelly considers himself a Gardnerian-tradition Witch.

Every month at the time of the full moon the group gathers to conduct their main ritual. This takes place with all the members "skyclad"—that is, nude. It begins with a dance, men and women rotating in a circle facing out. Everybody sings, "Thout-thout-a-tout-tout, throughout and about." The men put their weight only on the toes of their left feet, which gives them a hobbling gait. At a certain moment, the priestess breaks free and guides the others inward in a spiral. When she gets to the center, she kisses the man next to her and begins to unwind the spiral. Each woman then kisses each man, and the spiral opens up into a circle again. Kelly claims the dance is 6,000 years old and is symbolic of reincarnation.

Hearing of nude rituals inevitably leads one to ask, what part does sex play in witchcraft rites? Historically it was charged that witchcraft sabbats, or assemblies, always ended in wild orgies. Witches deny this, but they also stress that they do not possess the Christian attitude which regards sex as something evil. There is, for example, no witchcraft prohibition on premarital sex. Indeed, many witches think of marriage itself as irrelevant. There is a bit more disagreement about the actual use of sex in the rituals. Gavin Frost puts the matter rather delicately. "We value sex as pleasure, as the symbol and embodiment of life and as one of the sources of energies used in magical practice and religious worship." Others speak more enthusiastically of sex magic, and how sex liberates occult powers. Ritual sex is said to be the central ingredient in the Great Rite, one of the most sacred rituals of Gardnerian Witchcraft, and part of the initiation rite of Welsh traditional witchcraft.

Yet neither sex nor nudity is necessary in many Witchcraft groups. And all groups are wary of "swingers" who are simply looking for action. One Witch confided that if people wanted to join a coven just for the sex, they would soon discover that it was so infrequent that they would be very disappointed.

Drugs are another touchy subject. Historically there is a strong connection between witchcraft and drug use. Many of those accused of witchcraft during the Middle Ages were basically village magicians who dealt in herbal cures and other drugs. There is also considerable suspicion that some of the medieval witches used hallucination-producing substances, and that the tales of flying off to sabbats on brooms are the product of drugged fantasies. Modern witches, particularly those who talk about ecology and living "naturally," appear to discourage drug use not only in ceremonies but in personal life as well. Some young drug users have claimed that they are "witches," though most of the more orthodox witches would reject this claim. The whole movement is so disorganized that it is really impossible to generalize, though I would conclude that drugs do not seem to play much of a part in modern witchcraft.

How does one become a Witch? Witches say they do not proselytize because they belong to a secret religion. Most people become Witches by meeting initiated Witches and expressing an interest. Yet personal contact is not always necessary. In the April 21, 1974, issue of *Gnostica News,* the Council of American Witches lists coven openings in places as diverse as Manhattan and Iowa City, Iowa.

Requirements for membership vary greatly. Initiations are generally conducted with as much awesome ceremony as a particular coven can muster. Impressive initiations have been a popular feature of secret societies since ancient times. Even today the initiation rite of Masons retains a good deal of its old mysterious ritual. This ritual seems foolish in what has essentially become a businessman's society without real secrecy or magic, but at one time such rituals were deeply solemn and meaningful. Some witchcraft groups have various grades through which the initiate can progress. This is a practice more typical of occult groups and secret societies than most modern religions, but it was a practice not unknown in ancient mystery religions.

There is little in witchcraft theory to indicate that one must undergo some sort of religious or conversion experience comparable to baptism in the Holy Spirit. However, Gavin Frost says that an experience of that sort is really necessary before one can become a true Witch. "Without it," he says, "even if you're initiated you're just fooling around." John Ray speaks of making "breakthroughs" to greater levels of awareness, of an opening of the "cosmic consciousness."

The witchcraft rituals are often believed to provide some kind of mystical release, the kind of "peak experience" that followers in many other religions crave. Thus modern witchcraft is not merely a matter of spells and rituals, it is also to a degree an experience-oriented religion.

As a footnote to a discussion of modern witchcraft, we should look briefly at the subject of modern Paganism. Originally the word "pagan" meant anyone who worshiped the gods of the ancient

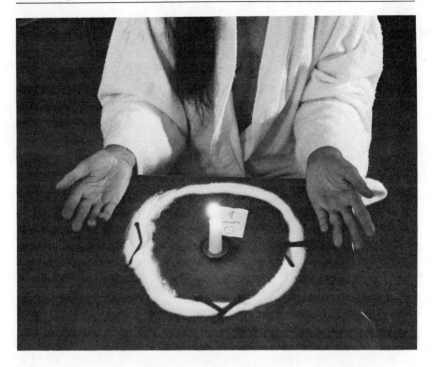

Ceremonial magic, like this spell designed to ward off unwanted attention, is an important part of modern Witchcraft.

Greeks and Romans. It later came to mean anyone who was not a Jew, Christian or Moslem, and more recently the term has been applied to anyone who is not particularly religious and leads a rather hedonistic life.

None of these definitions quite fits what is meant by modern Paganism. A modern Pagan is someone who claims to be the follower of a religious tradition that has either been secretly passed down through the ages, rediscovered, or just invented. Such traditions tend to be undogmatic and relatively free about things like sex and drugs. That sounds a great deal like a some descriptions of modern Witchcraft, but Witches themselves often speak of "Witches and Pagans" as if there were some sort of distinct and separate Pagan movement outside of general witchcraft and occultism.

Yet if such a movement really exists, it is extraordinarily hard to discern. The whole idea of modern Paganism appears to spring

primarily from the occultists' love of using several words where
one would do. Some people who are essentially practicing Witchcraft do not like to always call themselves Witches, so they call
themselves Pagans.

The situation can become quite confusing. For example, a bit
earlier we quoted Aidan Kelly's description of a Witchcraft ritual.
Kelly was actually the head of a group called the New Reformed
Orthodox Order of the Golden Dawn. That name was a deliberate
put-on, though the Golden Dawn was a British magical-occult society that flourished earlier in this century. Gerald Gardner was
associated with, or at least heavily influenced by, the Golden Dawn.
So the NROOGD has also been called a Gardnerian Witchcraft
group. Yet the group has become the center for a "Pagan Association," and it publishes a newsletter called *The Witches Trine*.

In the 1960s a man by the name of Tim Zell founded a group
he called the Church of All Worlds. It was based upon the mythology found in the popular science fiction novel *Stranger in a
Strange Land* by Robert Heinlein. The book had taken on cultic
significance to many high school and college students. Zell began
to invent his own form of Paganism, which he labeled Neo-Paganism, and published a journal called *The Green Egg*. To con-
fuse the issue further, Zell is also an initiated Witch.

Other more or less formal groups used the mythology of J. R. R.
Tolkien's *Lord of the Rings* trilogy as the center for their "Pagan"
religion. Still other groups have stressed Robert Graves' versions of
Greek religion, or the ideas of Aleister Crowley, a twentieth-century British occultist with a rather nasty reputation. We will look
at the influential Crowley more closely in our discussion of
Satanism.

In Britain there is a highly visible Druidic group that gets a lot
of publicity by performing their yearly ritual at Stonehenge. I was
unable to discover whether this group has a functioning American
branch, but I would not be surprised if it did.

On balance, though, Paganism, outside of Witchcraft or general
occult groups, does not appear to amount to a great deal at
present, and it is hard to decide how much of the little there is is
actually serious.

Satanism

The air is filled with rumors of secret "Satanic cults." Yet logically, Satanism should not exist, indeed cannot exist. Satanism has been called the reverse of Christianity. This definition, however, presents an insoluble problem. The Christian Devil—Satan—is not an evil god. He is not a god at all. Satan in orthodox Christian theology is another servant of God, one specially created as an instrument of temptation and punishment. In a sense, the warfare between Christ and Satan is a sham, since Satan is never out of God's control.

In the Old Testament, the prophet Amos recognized that evil was not the creation of Satan when he said, "Shall there be evil in a city and the Lord hath not done it?" To worship Satan in orthodox Christian terms is to worship a servant who has an unpleasant task to do, but not real power to grant any favors. To worship the biblical Satan is to condemn oneself to eternal damnation.

But Christianity did not develop in a vacuum. It was heavily influenced by many traditions other than Judaism. During early
Christian times there were a number of highly influential religious
systems which did not view all power as flowing from a single God.
The Gnostics, for example, believed that the God worshiped by
Christians was a usurper, and that there was a vastly more powerful, but unknown God whom they revered. *Gnosos,* the Greek
word for knowledge concerning this God, was possessed only by
a small group of initiates, and was held in secrecy.

Perhaps the most significant of the early heresies, as far as the
development of Satanism is concerned, was Manichaeism. The
Manichees saw the universe as a place of conflict between eternal
and equally powerful forces of good and evil. Manichaeism developed into a highly sophisticated body of religious thought that
was influenced by Christianity and highly attractive to many Christians as well. St. Augustine himself had at one time been a Mani-
chee. Not that the Manichaean sects were Devil worshipers or followers of the principle of evil. Indeed, they were a good deal more
ascetic and rigid than most of the Christians of their time. But at
least they recognized the possibility of competing but equal forces
of good and evil, and such a belief is almost a necessity if one is to
become a Devil worshiper.

It is also possible to read the New Testament and come away
with the distinct impression that Satan possesses a goodly measure
of independent power. Perhaps he is not an equal of God, but he
appears supreme on Earth, and able to grant his followers
earthly rewards. Christian theologians would, of course, deny this,
but most common folk were less interested in theology than simply in getting through life, and the appeal of a readily accessible,
though evil, earthly monarch as contrasted to an awesome, but
distant, and perhaps indifferent supreme God must have been great.
Many sincere Christians undoubtedly felt desperate enough to
risk eternal damnation in order to gain some measure of success
in this world. Others may have felt that through the use of magic
one could deal with the Devil and still not pay the eternal price, or
even that it wasn't wrong to ask the Devil for earthly rewards, so
long as one also paid attention to spiritual duties like attending

mass regularly. Today many good Christians also consult their astrological charts and feel no basic conflict.

However, the obstacles to deciding whether or not there ever was a large and organized historical Satanic movement are formidable. Surviving records from the days of early Christian supremacy through the end of the Middle Ages are almost exclusively church records. These documents describe the activities of a vast array of "Satanic" or "diabolical" groups. But can such records be believed? Churchmen habitually regarded all non-Christians, as well as many unorthodox Christians, as Devil worshipers. Witches, pagans, heretics, Jews and Moslems were all indiscriminately labeled Devil worshipers at one time or another. All were accused of a variety of abominable practices, from copulating with the Devil to sacrificing unbaptized infants. The Roman Catholic Church accused early Protestants of being servants of the Devil, and Protestants returned the accusation in kind. In such an atmosphere it is difficult to decide whether groups were diabolical, simply different or entirely imaginary.

It is quite likely that there were some organized groups in genuine revolt against the rigid structure of orthodox Christianity. As a sign of that revolt they may have paid homage to the Devil, defied traditional morality and performed perverted versions of Christian rituals. But the evidence indicates that if such groups existed at all, they were neither numerous nor well-organized. They drew their support largely from the desperate poor. But the whole problem is an academic one in any case, for most modern Satanists, unlike modern witches, are not particularly interested in proving the antiquity of their cult. They make few claims about being heirs of an unbroken ancient tradition.

The popular picture of Satanism, black mass and all, is drawn more from literary sources, like the works of the Marquis de Sade and other decadent writers. Another source for the popular image of Satanism were organizations like England's Hellfire Club, which flourished in the late eighteenth century. The Hellfire Club was typical of many groups labeled Satanist. It consisted of wealthy, bored young gentlemen who met together to dabble in magic, hold orgies and generally outrage the Christian establishment. They often dressed in black robes and performed obscene parodies of Christian rituals. Though there may have been serious students of magic and occultism among them, the primary purpose of the Hellfire Club appears to have been to have a good time and to shock people. It has been rumored that Benjamin Franklin attended meetings of the club while he was in England. This accusation cannot be proved, but it is not entirely impossible, for Franklin was neither a practicing Christian nor a moral puritan.

Another popular image for the modern Satanist was Aleister Crowley, the early-twentieth-century occultist. Crowley would certainly have never regarded himself as a Satanist, for he believed neither in God nor the Devil. He did, however, try to practice all sorts of magic ("magick" as he persistently spelled it). He was a great exponent of sex magic. In fact, he was a great exponent of sex: heterosexual, homosexual, group, ritual, public—any kind at all. Crowley was also a drug addict, a heavy drinker, a sadist, a monumental egotist and a publicity-seeking screwball. For years his well-reported exploits alternately titilated and shocked the readers of sensational newspapers throughout the world.

For all his notoriety Crowley never really had much of a following. But he was a very prolific writer, and many of the ceremonies, chants and rituals that he devised turn up today among groups that are called Satanist. Crowley was undoubtedly the model for the chief Satanist in *Rosemary's Baby*.

A major problem in assessing Crowley is trying to figure out when or even if he was serious, for he was known to have a wicked sense of humor, and was often forced to live by his wits. This involved selling a lot of magical hokum. My own suspicion is that Crowley believed very little of the nonsense he wrote. But serious or not, his influence lingers on and may well be growing.

The current Satanist scene is as murky as ever it was. There is a tremendous popular interest in the Devil, as shown by the astonishing success of the movie *The Exorcist* and the seriousness with which this rather ordinary Hollywood shocker is being discussed. Pope Paul VI created a worldwide sensation when in an address delivered in November 1972 he called the Devil, "a living spiritual being, perverted and perverting. A terrible reality. Mysterious and frightening."

Indeed, even before Pope Paul spoke, a survey indicated that belief in the reality of the Devil had grown over the past decade, while belief in God had declined. More people still believed in God than in the devil, but the gap had narrowed considerably.

The poll conducted by the Opinion Research Center of Chicago indicated that Americans' belief in the Devil has gone up from 37 per cent to 48 per cent since 1964, with another 20 per cent half-persuaded that the Devil exists. On the other hand, the proportion of those claiming to believe in God has gone down from 77 per cent to 69 per cent during the same ten years.

As in the past, some Christians seem ready to accuse practically everyone else of being a Satanist. We have already discussed how this operates in relation to witchcraft. There are rumors of secret and abominable rites being performed in abandoned churches and old graveyards. Newspapers frequently describe murders as "ritualistic," as though human sacrifice had become a widespread custom in America. On numerous occasions I have been told of Satanist cults, but all attempts to track them down have proved fruitless. Not that I doubt the existence of Satanist groups, but I do believe that there is more shadow than substance to the Satanist "movement." Some Satanists, however, have "come out of the closet" and "gone public."

Bonewits divides Satanists into Liberals and Conservatives. "Think of the matter in political terms," he advises, "for the religions are very much what you would get if you tried to turn Right Wing and Left Wing political philosophies into theology." The distinction is a useful one.

Bonewits continues:

> These [Liberal] Satanists are mostly young people, in-
> intellectuals and hippies, who have never heard of the
> word "Pagan" so they have to call themselves *something*.
> Where a Conservative Satanist is fascist in politics, a
> Liberal Satanist is anarchistic and more relaxed and less
> self-conscious in his hedonism. Liberal Satanism involves
> drug taking and occasionally ritual murder; for while the
> Conservative Satanists seldom believe what they're doing
> enough to take the concept of human sacrifice seriously,

the Liberal Satanists are often so very stoned and so very
desperate for new kicks that they are perfectly willing to
go all the way in their beliefs.

The best-known and probably the largest Satanist group in the
U.S. today is the Church of Satan, with headquarters in San Francisco and headed by Anton Szandor LaVey. LaVey is no secret
Satanist. He courts publicity, and very successfully, too. He first
came to public notice when Jayne Mansfield, one of the many Hollywood imitators of Marilyn Monroe, joined the Church of Satan.
LaVey had a dispute with her boy friend, and when both were
killed in an auto accident the rumor spread that LaVey had cursed
them. LaVey claims that he only cursed the boy friend. "She
brought about her own demise. But it wasn't through what I had
done to curse *her*."

LaVey's greatest public relations coup to date came when he
served as "technical adviser" and bit-part player in the film *Rosemary's Baby*. He says that the film has given the Church of Satan
a tremendous boost.

LaVey, who spent years working in carnivals and did a stint as
an employee of the San Francisco police department, started his
Church of Satan in 1966. It grew from small informal classes in
occultism that he had been running. Today the Church of Satan
boasts well over 10,000 members, and La Vey's books, like the
Satanic Bible, are occult best sellers. LaVey's followers often call
him "the Black Pope," and he plays his part with gusto. He shaves
his head, sports a pointed Vandyke beard, and during ceremonies
wears a black cape and a skullcap with horns. The Church of Satan
is also very much a LaVey family business. His wife is high priestess, while his teen-age daughter describes herself as a "compleat
witch"—the name of another LaVey book.

The regular Friday night rituals of the Church of Satan are
theatrically impressive. The room is dark and an organ plays eerie
music. Candles are lit, revealing robed figures. The male participants wear black robes and hoods resembling those worn by the
Ku Klux Klan. The women wear robes without hoods. Officiating
over the assemblage is LaVey himself in his Devil costume.

Anton Szandor LaVey

Writer Arthur Lyons describes what happens next.

> A bell is rung nine times to signal the beginning of the
> service, the priest turning in a circle counterclockwise,
> ringing the bell to the four cardinal points. The leopard-
> skin cover is removed from the mantelpiece, revealing
> the nude body of the female volunteer altar for the eve-
> ning. . . .LaVey then takes a sword from its sheath, held
> by Diane, his wife and high priestess, and invokes Satan
> in his cardinal manifestations. Satan, in the South, repre-
> sents Fire; Lucifer, in the East, is symbolic of Air; Belial,
> in the North, represents Earth; and Leviathan, in the
> West, is his watery aspect. The officiating priest then
> drinks from the Chalice, which is filled with any liquid
> he may desire, from lemonade to 100 proof vodka, mak-
> ing a symbolic offering to Satan.

Ceremonies vary considerably. Often members of the congregation come forward and are asked what they desire. This may be
anything from money to the destruction of an enemy. The priest
then touches the member's head with a sword, and asks the Devil
to grant the wish. Then priests and members focus all of their emotional force on attaining the wish.

The nude girl as an altar is a standard feature of the infamous
black mass, which is more a literary than a religious creation. The
sword, bells, candles, cardinal points and the various symbols that
adorn the room are taken from many branches of occultism. There
is, however, one basic flaw in the entire ritual—Anton LaVey does
not believe in the Devil.

To LaVey and his followers Satan is not a supernatural being.
Certainly the Devil is not "a living spiritual being" as described by
the pope. Satan for these Satanists is merely a symbol of the desire
for self-gratification which exists in all of us. This, says LaVey, is
our "true nature," and it is the purpose of his church to recognize
this nature and glorify it.

Christianity, he believes, perverts this true nature, and much of
LaVey's theology consists of upside-down Christianity. "Blessed

are the strong, for they shall possess the earth. If a man smite you
on one cheek, SMASH him on the other!" he writes in his *Satanic
Bible*.

"We recognize," LaVey says, "that man is sometimes lower than
the animals, that he is basically greedy and selfish, so why feel
guilty about it? We accept ourselves as we are and live with it. The
one great sin is self-deceit."

What about the afterlife, eternal damnation? LaVey isn't interested. It is the here and now that interests him. Indeed, he is
absolutely scornful of those who believe in the supernatural, evil or
otherwise.

But the Church of Satan is not completely materialist, for it does
hold that each individual possesses some sort of power within himself with which he can bend nature to his will if the power is fo-
cused properly. That is the stated purpose of the rituals and all of the
magical trappings. LaVey sees the power as some sort of natural
biological force, though there is no proof such a force exists at all.
This view, which is very close to Aleister Crowley's view of magic,
is quite common in modern occult circles. Many of the "white
witches" of the Gardnerian school would doubtless be in basic
agreement with this view of magic and the need for ritual.

While the horns, hoods and nude girl are the showiest aspects
of the Church of Satan, its basic appeal appears to lie in LaVey's
well-advertised lack of hypocrisy. Time after time interviewers
have described him as being "refreshingly candid." For example,
many cult leaders are extremely embarassed and evasive about the
way they get their funds, and what is done with the money. LaVey
admits that membership in his church can be expensive (though it
isn't necessarily). He says that the Church of Satan is worth every
penny, and besides, his followers can afford whatever fee he
charges. He openly courts the affluent, for he says that Satanists
are not interested in "losers." One definition of a loser is someone
who cannot afford to join the Church of Satan. LaVey spends whatever he thinks is needed running his church, and the rest goes into
his personal bank account. Anyone who doesn't like the arrange-
ment can quit.

Status-seeking, often denounced by other religious organizations, is encouraged in LaVey's church. One rises in the church hierarchy not only by proficiency in Satanism, but also by his "dining preferences," the "style of decor" of his home and the "make, year and condition" of his automobile, according to a report on the Church of Satan in *Time* magazine.

LaVey has nothing but contempt for those he calls "tea shoppe witches," nor does he care for dropouts and hippies, whom he lumps in that large class of losers. He insists that the Church of Satan carefully screens applicants in order to weed out the "nuts" who apply for membership in great numbers. The membership of the Church of Satan does appear to be quite respectable in a thoroughly conventional way. It runs heavily to professional military men, policemen, technicians and low-level executives. LaVey has had a few celebrity converts, like Jayne Mansfield, but in this area his appeal is far behind that of the more popular Eastern gurus.

The Church of Satan clearly falls within Bonewits' definition of Conservative Satanists. Politically LaVey is a supporter of George Wallace. He denounces many black leaders as "loud baboons," and is an outspoken advocate of "law and order."

"We haven't been hassled too much by the law," he says, "because we have so many policemen in our organization. I'm an ex-cop myself . . . and I've maintained my contacts. They've provided for me a kind of security force. But all in all, we have a very clean slate. We are very evil outlaws in theological circles, but not in civil."

Drugs, while not specifically condemned by the Church of Satan, are viewed with extreme disfavor, for they cause a "loss of control." There is a great deal of verbal violence in Church of Satan services, but physical violence is not openly advocated. While LaVey discusses human sacrifice in his *Satanic Bible,* he is not talking about actually going out and stabbing anyone. He writes, "The use of a human sacrifice in a Satanic ritual does not imply that the sacrifice is slaughtered 'to appease the gods.' *Symbolically,* the victim is destroyed through the working of a hex or curse, which in turn leads to the physical, mental or emotional destruction of the 'sacrifice' in ways not attributable to the magician." Church of

Satan services often end with the whole congregation sitting around cursing people.

LaVey does not advocate the sacrifice of babies or animals; indeed, the very thought horrifies him. Satanists, he says, are the only ones who possess real respect for life and the human body. Children and animals are entirely "natural" and "unhypocritical" and thus in the view of the Church of Satan are "natural Satanists."

A Satanist should sacrifice, by symbolic means, of course, "Anyone who has unjustly wronged you—one who has 'gone out of his way' to hurt you—to deliberately cause trouble and hardship for you or those dear to you. In short, a person who is asking to be cursed by their very actions."

The followers of the Church of Satan whom I have talked to are passionately attached to their doctrine. One became so angry at something I had once written about "Dr." LaVey that he said he and his friends would "rather read the Holy Bible" than any of my books. Others say that they have really been helped by the Church of Satan, by being freed of their guilt feelings and allowed to recognize their "true selves."

Yet the Church of Satan strikes outsiders, at least this outsider, as unusually banal. There is nothing either surprising or deep about LaVey's view of human nature. Advocates of self-gratification without guilt have been around in great numbers for a long time. The only things which set the Church of Satan apart from the mass of ordinary pleasure-seekers and power-seekers are the magical trappings, which in themselves are neither particularly original nor startling. There lingers about these rituals the air of a B-rated horror film.

And there is a deeper paradox. LaVey scorns "losers" and says he attracts only the successful to his church. This is a good sales point, for if one joins it gives him a feeling of being part of a successful elite. Yet the Satanists of whom LaVey boasts represent at best the respectable middle class, not the conspicuously successful. And what about the rest of the members? One might well imagine that the Church of Satan contains its share of the frustrated and unsuccessful, and it provides for them an outlet through which they can harmlessly strike back at a society that has largely ignored them. Its main appeal may be therapeutic rather than religious or magical.

There is a widespread suspicion, that the entire Church of Satan is nothing but a joke, or worse, a con game. LaVey insists that it is neither, and many who have met him are convinced he is sincere. More significantly, thousands upon thousands of Americans—good solid Americans—are drawn to LaVey's vision of humanity, and to his particular brand of black magic.

One can hardly discuss modern Satanism without mentioning Charles Manson, whose "family" carried out a number of hideously spectacular "ritual" murders in California in 1970. Manson, who occasionally called himself Satan as well as Christ, is a good example of Bonewits' Liberal Satanist. The Manson group were heavy drug users, and they did go all the way to human sacrifice, apparently for kicks rather than from any mystical religious or ritualistic reason.

Manson dabbled in all kinds of occultism (as, by the way, did Robert Kennedy's assassin, Sirhan Sirhan), but drugs and quite possibly insanity complicate the picture. Most of Manson's statements were illogical to the point of incoherence. He apparently had no consistent philosophy of Satanism, or of anything else. In fact, he is labeled a Satanist primarily because he did evil things, and Satanists are supposed to do evil things. Another connection appears to have been that one of his group's murder victims was Sharon Tate, wife of Roman Polanski, the man who directed the film *Rosemary's Baby*.

Some observers have blamed the Manson family murders and a number of other murders, primarily in California, on "Satanism" or a climate of "evil occultism." I am personally inclined to doubt the power of Satanism or any other form of evil occultism to drive people to the extreme of murder. It may give murderously inclined individuals a framework in which to commit their acts, and an excuse of sorts for them, but it is not the motive force. Is Christianity to be blamed because someone obeying what he believes to be the voice of God murders his family to save them from "eternal damnation"?

Aside from Anton LaVey's Church of Satan, there appear to be no large or well-organized Satanic groups. There are many small occult groups which dabble in an Aleister Crowley type of black magic, but while such groups may indulge in quite nasty practices, they cannot specifically be called Satanic.

There are also an unknown number of distinctly pathological groups like the Charles Manson "family," but we hear very little about them unless they burst spectacularly into public view because of some crime they have committed.

According to Arthur Lyons, "The more militant, sado-masochistic groups attract a more deviant, antisocial membership. The inner workings of these groups have been little investigated by researchers into the subject because of the often justifiable fear of the investigator of foul play." But though there are plenty of rumors, there is no hard evidence that such groups are numerous or that they possess any consistent Satanic philosophy.

Modern Satanism, therefore, seems to be pretty much what Satanism has always been, more a rebellion against traditional values than a viable religion. Often it is little more than a semiserious excuse for doing what one would probably do anyway, and that could be anything from cheating in business to murder. Calling something Satanic gives the forbidden a little extra spice. Most of all, though, Satanism's present, like Satanism's past, is grossly exaggerated.

The Process/The Foundation

Along with about fifty other persons I found myself sitting cross-legged on a cushion in a house in a modestly tacky section of Toronto, Canada. At the back of the room was a small musical group —a couple of guitars, a flute, some drums and a small gong. In front was a wooden table, a lectern, and hanging on the wall a large silver-colored cross emblazoned with a fierce-looking red serpent.

Most of the others in the room were young, in their late teens or early twenties, and might roughly be described as student-types. We had all been given books containing hymns and a detailed description of the ceremony in which we were about to partake, though the majority had clearly been at similar ceremonies before and knew the hymns by heart.

The gong was struck and a small procession entered the room from the rear. The leader was a striking-looking woman wearing a green robe and carrying a bowl in which a fire was blazing. She was followed by a bearded man in a red robe and three other women wearing blue uniforms and a small replica of the cross with the serpent around their necks. They were singing about Christ and Satan.

This was the regular Saturday evening Sabbath Assembly of the Process Church of the Final Judgment. The same ceremony was taking place in cities throughout the United States.

Before attending the Process service I had told friends half-jokingly that I was going to a Devil worshipers' black mass. What I found was no secret cult of drug-taking Devil worshipers, but one of the most curious, and curiously attractive, of all the unorthodox religions in America.

But the Devil worshipers charge has been leveled against the Process so often that we must deal with it at once. The charge probably first grew out of the Process' own theology. Processeans worship four Gods, or four aspects of God. They are Jehovah, the God of vengeance, but also of courage and self-denial, duty and purity; and Lucifer, representative of enjoyment and kindness but also descending into greed and jealousy. Satan, the third God, has two poles in Process thought. On the one side he is representative of lust, violence and excess; on the other, detachment, mysticism and asceticism. Standing somewhat apart from these three Great Gods is Christ the Unifier, the Gods' link with the human race. These Gods are real spiritual entities, not just abstractions or vague nonpersonal forces.

The Process holds that all of the different qualities represented in the Gods are present in all of us, though to different degrees. We each have our own individual "God patterns." One of the aims of the Process is to get us to recognize these different qualities in ourselves and others, and to try to reduce conflicts that the contending forces produce. A favorite Process precept runs:

> Christ said: Love your enemies.
> Christ's Enemy was Satan and Satan's Enemy was Christ.
> Through Love enmity is destroyed.
> Through Love saint and sinner destroy the enmity between them.

Now this is a partial and woefully incomplete exposition of Process theology, which becomes quite elaborate and is constantly changing. One can argue with the Process on philosophical, moral, theological, practical and even national grounds. But even so, one can not fairly conclude that this is the theology of a group of sex- and violence-obsessed Devil worshipers. The Process tries to confront the problem of evil in the world which has vexed so many religions. It does not encourage evil.

Central to the Process belief is what they call the Universal Law: "As you give so shall you receive." Processeans do volunteer work in hospitals and other institutions, run free kitchens for the poor and coffee houses for street people, offer counseling for the troubled, take care of animals and engage in a lot of other social service activities. Robert Flavin, coordinator of volunteers at Willowbrook, an understaffed and overcrowded home for the retarded in New York State, said of Process volunteers, "They're not fair-weather volunteers. I wish I had a thousand like them." Volunteer work at Willowbrook is neither pleasant nor easy, and it is hardly the sort of thing that hedonists would enjoy.

And yet, when one mentions Satan, and sees that red serpent, all of the old images of the black mass, orgies, and infant sacrifice immediately come to mind. And Process precepts like "The surest way to become susceptible to the power of evil is to resist it" seem to be diabolical in the most commonly understood sense of the word. The Process contends that evil should be controlled rather than resisted. The distinction between resistance and control is, however, a bit too subtle for some non-Processeans.

The greatest public relations blow that the Process in America has received was when they were identified as a major influence on Charles Manson. This charge was made in a popular book on the Manson case, and excerpts from the book were printed in a mass-circulation national magazine. The Process sued, and the author admitted that he made a mistake. The magazine printed a retraction. That helped, but some of the mud has stuck nonetheless. Father Joab, Superior at the Process chapter in Toronto, believes that the charge first originated with another cult that bore a grudge against the Process and sent this false information to the press.

No one but the most doctrinaire fundamentalist Christian could get Devil worship out of current Process activities. Processeans say that they have little trouble with their neighbors or with the police. Occasionally they have run-ins with Jesus People, particularly members of the Children of God, but Processeans do not seek out such confrontations. Despite these problems, the Process magazine printed a highly sympathetic article about the Children of God.

At one time, though, the Process was a much scarier-looking group. But Process thinking and activity is always evolving. That is, in fact, the meaning of the name Process. A few years ago the Processeans wore ominous-looking black uniforms and, instead of a cross, used a goat-headed insignia, the very symbol of Satan. They were also more exclusive, suspicious, and less open about their ideas. They even refused to talk to the press. But the approach didn't work, says Father Joab, so it was changed.

A brochure put out by the Process describes it as "A religious order; a Church at the core of which is a group of highly trained and dedicated people who have spent several years in mainly experimental work; developing, discovering, trying and testing all the basic principles, methods and tenets upon which the Process is founded."

In May of 1974 a very revolutionary development took place in the evolution of the Process. There was a major schism, and the name of the church was changed from The Process Church of the Final Judgment to The Foundation Church of the Millennium.

The change came about as the result of a dispute between the group's ruling body, the Council of Masters, and Robert de Grimston, founder of the Process. De Grimston lost, though he apparently still leads a small group called the Process. All of the major Process centers and the vast majority of the members have gone over to the Foundation.

The chief point of dispute appears to have been the doctrine of the Unity of Christ and Satan. One of the original Process members, Father Micah, told a reporter for the *New York Post,* "We finally admitted that the doctrine of loving Satan never made much sense. . . . It was like deciding to have a tooth pulled. It hurt, but if we didn't do it the whole jaw might rot."

"It's an elegant mental construction," said Micah. "But it really does take a quantum leap to get from loving your enemies to loving Satan." When loving Satan was part of Process doctrine, the Satanist image continued to get in the way and cause confusion.

The ultimate results of this change are impossible to judge at this writing. At the very least they mean new symbols and rituals. The Sabbath Assembly that I described at the beginning of this chapter is now called a Sabbath Celebration. There is no more talk of Christ and Satan, but the general form and feeling of the meeting remain the same. The cross with the scarlet snake has given way to a double F symbol enclosed in a Star of David. The Council of Masters is now the Council of Luminaries, and the formal Process greeting, "As it is, so be it," has been changed to "Shalom." There is little talk of "the gods" now and more concentration on Jehovah. "In a way we are very Jewish without being Jewish," says Father Joab.

Church members view the change as more of a counterreformation than a revolution, a return to the basic principles upon which the Process was founded. This means more stress on the end of the world, which the Foundation believes is coming very soon. They also believe in the coming of a Messiah, though they have no fixed ideas about the form in which he (or possibly she) will arrive. The Messiah, they say, will establish the millennium—a thousand years of peace and love. The Foundation sees itself as dedicated to the establishment and construction of a secure base for the beginnings of this new era, and works toward this end.

At present it appears as though these changes, though major and even traumatic to members of the group, will not greatly affect their activities as far as the outside world is concerned, or even their own personal lifestyles. They are viewed as changes in form rather than basic substance.

But, of course, one can never be sure, so most of what is discussed in this section refers to the Process as it was up to the time of the change to the Foundation in May 1974. I will continue to describe the group as the Process, except where I am specifically describing events that took place after the change.

The Satanism charge had long hounded the Process, and Foundation members hope that they will finally be able to get Satan behind them. In a book on Satanism in America writer Arthur Lyons said of the Process:

> Savage and indiscriminate sex is forced on the entrants into the cult not as a means of religious communion but as a means of purging the initiates of any residual of Grey Forces that might be latent in them. [Grey Forces represent hypocrisy, intolerance, and a lot of other negative things in traditional society.] Sex is a means of cutting members off from the outside and subjecting them to the will of the group, or the will of the group leaders.

Father Joab's reaction to this charge was, "But we're celibate!" He explained that marriage is allowed within the Process, but that unmarried ministers must remain celibate. Process ministers live communally, and the reason for celibacy is, they say, not because they disapprove of sex, but simply because it makes for a smoother running community. Though the Processeans that I talked to didn't seem to be aware of it, history bears them out. The most successful communal groups—monastic orders and the Shakers in America—have been celibate. For some reason, free love rarely makes for a successful commune.

Children are born into the Process. At the Sabbath Assembly that I attended there were about half a dozen youngsters, mostly under five. All were wearing the dark clothes and silver serpent crosses of the Process.

How could anyone have ever gotten the idea that there was some sort of sexual initiation in the Process? Brother Amos of the New York City chapter said that it might have come from the earlier days of the Process, when they stressed "the negativity and violence latent in everyone." But the charge that savage sex, or any kind of sex, was ever forced on initiates he rejected utterly. Every initiate into the higher orders of the Process must abstain from sexual relations as part of the preparation for initiation.

While some of the Jesus People appear obsessed with, if hostile to, sex, and some of the Oriental religions try to ignore sex entirely, the Process takes an astonishingly liberal position. For example, a spring 1974 issue of the Process magazine contains a highly sympathetic article on the New York Dolls, a transvestite freak rock group that is currently as popular among teen-agers as it is shocking to their parents.

The Process disapproves of drugs, but does not condemn the drug user (or anyone else) as lost. Processeans also do not drink alcohol except on some ceremonial occasions.

The second part of the Process title, Church of the Final Judgment, now Church of the Millennium, indicates the profoundly apocalyptic nature of the group. Like so many other sects, the Process doesn't believe that the world as we know it is going to be around very much longer. Like many others, they also see the end coming around the year 2000. Processeans draw upon a whole variety of predictions to arrive at this date—Biblical prophecy, Nostradamus, the statements of modern psychics like Jean Dixon, and Edgar Cayce, and presumably upon prophetic visions within their own group. The prevailing view is that the end will come through conflict, probably nuclear war.

But while Processeans are quite sure that the end is near, they are not at all sure what this end is going to be. Nor do they see the end of the world as the final end of everything. Rather, they see it as the start of a New Age. One of the Process precepts is, "He that endures to the End shall be part of the New Beginning."

Again and again it was stressed that no one really knows what is going to happen at the end or what the New Age is to be like. Brother Amos talked of the possibility of a new civilization "without fear, prejudice, all those negative things." Mother Mercedes, director of the New York center, said it might be possible that the New Age would be one in which individuals would exist "in spirit only."

At one point during the development of the Process the end of the world idea was pressed very hard, and the Foundation will again emphasize the end, but for a while it was played down. "People tend to back away from the Final Judgment part," Mother Mercedes said. Even when it was de-emphasized, the end of the world concept was never abandoned. Father Joab has collected a

Mother Rhea leads a Sabbath Assembly, the most important of the weekly religious meetings of the Foundation.

whole mass of *Predictions for the End* into an anthology published by the Process. "We have no illusions about the state of the world," says Process literature. But while most of those who are convinced that the end is near become quite fanatic on the subject, Father Joab is surprisingly undogmatic.

I pointed out to him that every generation has believed that it is the last generation, and that they had all been wrong. What would he do, I asked, if the end didn't come.

"You mean if the sky rolled back like a scroll, there was a big laugh, and then it rolled closed again?"

"Even worse, what if there was no laugh, nothing, and the world just continued on its same miserable way?"

"I'm quite prepared for that. We realize that we could always be wrong."

Implicit in most apocalyptic visions is the idea that a certain remnant will be saved, while the rest, those who refuse to recognize the visionaries' truth, will be condemned to destruction, death, eternal damnation, or whatever. The believers will somehow or other get through.

Process founder De Grimston wrote some rather hair-raising things about the coming end:

> The distant rumblings that are heralds of the End have become a mighty roar closing in about us, piercing our eardrums and causing the very Earth to quake beneath our feet, so that very soon even the blindest, numbest, most oblivious of us will no longer be able to shut out the sound of it.
>
> By then the whole world will be stricken by the sound of its own approaching doom. Every man will gaze in horror at his fellow man, and see his own fear reflected back to him.
>
> And by then we must be free if we are ever to be free. By then the bonds that bind us must be broken, and we must stand above the terror of the End, aloof, detached, a part of something new.
>
> For with every end there is a new beginning, and if we are not of the End then we shall be of the New Beginning.

A basic Process brochure gives as the main purpose of the Process the building of a structure that will survive the coming destruction. "That structure, we of the Process are endeavoring to build; collecting our people, planting the seeds of a new way of life, which must come when the old has passed away."

This conjures up in my mind a sort of science fiction picture, in which the blue-uniformed Processeans emerge from the ruins of the world's cities as the only individuals intact and sane after the thermonuclear holocaust. Perhaps Processeans have the same picture in their heads. In any case it is a fairly standard apocalyptic vision.

The Process, however, does not condemn all non-Processeans to an eternity of suffering after death. "We think everyone is going to be saved," Father Joab said, "but that doesn't mean there isn't going to be a whole lot of suffering at the end." But he could not envision a universe in which a small percentage went to heaven and the vast majority spent eternity in hell. None of these views appear to have been altered by the schism.

The Process began in England in the mid-1960s. "We never set out to be a church at all. Ten years ago, we were simply a group of people gathered around one very charismatic figure," Father Micah said.

That figure was a young architecture student named Robert de Grimston Moor, who eventually became known as Robert de Grimston. "All of us had been experimenting with different psychologies and religions," Micah said. "It seemed clear to us, even then, that man was on a self-destructive course, and we wanted to find some way out."

"We included five architects, as well as students and other professionals. We'd been meeting for over a year as a sort of self-therapy group, when one night Robert began to reveal strange dreams he'd been having."

From these "strange dreams" grew the elaborate Process theology. In 1966 De Grimston, his wife Mary Ann, and a group of thirty others were deeply committed enough to leave their careers in England and retire to a small Mexican fishing village to develop their ideas. A year later they were ready to go out into the world to spread their ideas.

They chose America rather than their native England as the base for most of their activities. Though they have made many American converts, the group still retains an indefinable British character, and a high percentage of leaders come from that original group of thirty.

Since the Process has been around for about ten years, its leaders are older and have been with the group longer than those involved in many of the other unorthodox religious movements. The membership in general seems more stable. Observers of other unorthodox groups have said that members stick with a group on an average of two years, but the Process appears to have compiled a better record. There are dropouts and defectors, but Mother Mercedes insisted these were mostly at the lower levels—those who had not been with the Process very long. The change to the Foundation does not appear to have produced a large number of defections.

Until the May 1974 schism, De Grimston appeared to be the ing force behind the Process. His writings made up a large part of the many Process publications, and his picture, in various Christ-like attitudes, appeared frequently in these publications. De Grimston portraits also occupied prominent places on the walls of various Process centers. Yet De Grimston was neither worshiped like a god, as is the Guru Maharaj Ji, nor was he a hidden but all-powerful dictator, like David Berg of the Children of God. Processeans called De Grimston the leader and teacher and they revered him. He did not court publicity nor apparently grant interviews to outsiders. He did travel around a good deal to various Process centers giving guidance. But he did not exercise one-man control, for in his dispute with the Council of Masters, it was the Masters who won out. "Just because he looked like Jesus didn't mean he could walk on water, "one member told the *New York Post* reporter.

Most people's introduction to the Process or the Foundation comes through the street ministry. Anyone who regularly walked down New York's Fifth Avenue, Chicago's Michigan Avenue or near Boston's Harvard Square was almost certain to meet a blue-garbed minister selling literature. Process proselytizers, incidentally, are a good deal more polite than most proselytizers, and their literature is of a more professional quality, though often it is not particularly informative.

Anyone interested in the group can go to one of the coffee houses attached to most of the centers. These are very informal. People can sit around and have coffee and sometimes food. Donations to pay for the food are requested, but not pressed. At times there is music or other forms of entertainment. In keeping with the low key approach to to proselytizing, members do not immediately assault any new face that appears at a coffee house. If you want to be left alone or play a quiet game of chess, it is possible.

Anyone who follows the teachings of the Process in any way can consider himself a Processean as far as the church is concerned.

He would never even have to visit a headquarters or attend a ceremony. Mother Mercedes estimated that there were hundreds of thousands of such individuals in America. Their only physical connection with the Process was buying literature on the street.

But there is a more formal way of joining. One can become an Initiate by attending a Sabbath Assembly twice in a row and going through a very simple ceremony. The next step might be to become a Disciple, and this is a bit more complicated. (The names of all the ranks have been changed by the Foundation, but the system remains the same.) One must spend at least eight weeks as an Initiate, and go through various preparatory meetings, before being baptized as a Disciple. Once a Disciple, an individual can wear the uniform and symbols of the church and take part in various church projects. Disciples are in essence lay ministers, and are expected to contribute to the maintenance of the church by tithing approximately 10 per cent of their income. There are also what are called Field Disciples, persons who do not live near any Process center, but still wish to participate in some formal way in the activities of the church.

But there is another road, and that is to become a full-time minister. The first step is to become a Messenger. According to a Process publication, those chosen to become Messengers must show "a high degree of responsibility, self-discipline and self-control, be available for full-time work for the Church and attend Process activities." Once baptized a Messenger, the individual takes a new name, one of his or her own chosing, and the title Brother or Sister. Messengers who don't have their own funds are supported by the church.

At this stage, Messengers are often referred to as training ministers. They do not live with the regular ministers until they have served an apprenticeship of anywhere from six months to a year. Only then are they considered "Inside Processeans," or what are now called "The Elect."

What do insiders do? Says a Process recruiting brochure, "Well that's when the training really starts. But that's another story."

Such a statement is deliberately enigmatic, for it is not made clear what the "story" or the "training" is. Apparently as one moves into the higher ranks of the church there is a good deal of discussion of theology and practice. Whether the Process possesses or ever possessed some sort of "secret doctrine" revealed only to initiates of a certain rank, who are sworn to secrecy, is unknown. Such a practice, however, is fairly commonly in hierarchical religious organizations. There are certain documents meant only for Inside Processeans. A Process book called *Exit* by Robert de Grimston was originally meant only for Inside Processeans, but is now offered for sale to the general public.

The next step in the Process hierarchy is that of Prophet. One advances to this rank by displaying the proper personal qualities. A frequently mentioned quality is self-control. Above the Prophets are the Superiors. A Superior may also attain the position of Director of one of the Process headquarters, an added responsibility. At this rank one also assumes the title Mother or Father, rather than Brother or Sister.

Finally there is the rank of Master. The Council of Masters exercises tremendous control over the church. In mid-1974 there were eleven members of the Council of Masters, and they worked closely with founder De Grimston until the dispute which saw the end of the Process and the beginning of the Foundation. The Masters then changed their name to the Council of Luminaries.

For all the titles and ranks, there are only between one and two hundred Process ministers or Inside Processeans in the whole of North America. In the New York office about twenty of them lived communally in a building across the street from their headquarters. There were, in addition, seven training ministers who did not live with the regular ministers. The New York headquarters was the largest in North America. The Council of Masters had a separate building of their own in the New York area. By late 1974, the Foundation appeared to be concentrating its efforts more and more in New York.

The Process does not pretend to be completely democratic within its hierarchy. The Masters set major policy and choose or approve all who are to become Superiors or Directors. Those in the lower ranks look to those above for guidance. At any gathering, it is quite obvious that there are those who give orders and those who take them. Yet I was assured that blind obedience to leadership was not part of the Process, and that there was a good deal of interchange of ideas between those lower in the hierarchy and those above. Lower-level ministers, however, were unaware of the dispute between De Grimston and the Masters, and shocked by the split.

The Process holds a number of regular weekly ceremonies that are open to the public. In addition to the formal Sabbath Assembly that I described briefly at the beginning of this section, there is also a regular Process Forum for spreading the teachings of the church. There are evenings devoted to Process music (some of it quite good) and an evening set aside for healing. In its wanderings through things spiritual, the Process has hit upon spiritual healing as an important phenomena, and they say that they have seen many miraculous physical healings. In addition to healing by traditional means like laying on of hands, Processeans also regard good nutrition as part of healing. They are big on vitamins and natural foods. Yet oddly, for individuals so involved with health, many Processeans smoke, some very heavily. This is particularly striking after one has visited with other unorthodox religious groups which generally ban smoking.

When I pointed out the apparent contradiction between preaching the use of natural foods for health and smoking cigarettes, Mother Mercedes replied, "We believe that a little bit of what you fancy is good for you." It seemed typical of the Processeans' nondogmatic attitude toward life.

While the Process leaned heavily toward healing in mid-1974, and this emphasis was continued by the Foundation, they have at times stressed other aspects of the paranormal. Sessions in telepathy development used to be part of regular Process services. Process members still believe in telepathy. "We use only one-tenth of our mind," Father Joab told me. "We have fantastic powers locked up unused." But telepathy is no longer emphasized.

It is not the ceremonies, the music or the theology that impresses one most about the Process; it is the people. In the first place, they are physically attractive. I don't know why Inside Processeans are generally better looking than members of other groups, but they are. When I mentioned this impression to several Processeans, they thanked me for the compliment, but said that they could think of no reason for it.

The appearance of Processeans is helped considerably by the sharp uniforms and dramatic but tasteful crosses, rings and other symbols that they wear. Male Processeans seem to favor moderately long hair and beards (as did founder De Grimston). Both beards and hair are carefully trimmed. The women do not favor any particular hair style, but their hair is invariably tasteful and neat.

In sharp contrast to the rather shabby colony of the Children of God, or the nondescript offices of the Divine Light Mission, the New York City headquarters of the Process looks expensive in a functional and understated sort of way. It reminded me of the offices of a small but rising advertising agency.

This impression was heightened considerably after a visit to the rooms in which the Process produces its very slick publications. The Process stresses that members are encouraged to use their talents to the fullest, whatever these talents may be. In New York City, Process talents ran to commercial art and design.

Processeans dress well, and apparently live well. Sometimes on missionary jaunts they have endured hardship, but they do not look undernourished. The prices for property in East 38th Street, where the Process' New York office and communal dwelling are located, are very high. This raises the question of where Process gets its money. I was told that tithing and small donations make up part of the funds, but that people are not pressed to contribute, though some are said to be "extremely generous." A large portion of funds, say the Processeans, comes from the sale of their literature. Frankly, this is hard for me to believe, because I know that it is difficult to get rich, or even get along, in publishing, no matter how much volunteer labor you have. Perhaps the Processeans are simply good managers, or have wealthy backers, or maybe they are deeply in debt. The subject of Process financing is still a puzzle to me.

One of the more pleasant surprises in visiting the Process is that one always finds animals wandering about. The Process is very big on animals. One of their publications, called *The Ultimate Sin,* is an angry diatribe against scientific experimentation on animals. The Process appears to prefer large German shepherds to other dogs, and in the early days, when they were presenting a grimmer face to the outside world, some found the black-clad Processeans with their large and formidable-looking dogs sinister indeed. The dogs I found at the headquarters were more friendly than formidable, and at the Toronto headquarters there was a beautiful and unusually affectionate Siamese cat.

Most of all, though, Processeans talk well. They are intelligent and quite willing, even eager, to discuss anything that one cares to bring up. They appear to treat discussion with outsiders as an opportunity for a genuine interchange of ideas rather than as a nuisance which gets in the way of their real business, which is converting the outsider. A discussion does not degenerate into a string of stock phrases and quotes.

For a group that has a rather dismal view of the world and its immediate future, they possess considerable good humor. During the Sabbath Assembly I attended there was a moment when the musicians simply couldn't follow the melody they were supposed to be playing. After a few horrendously off-key notes the whole place broke up in laughter. And this was in the midst of what was supposed to be a solemn ceremony. Processeans are, in short, pleasantly nonfanatical.

Perhaps it is not really fair to compare the Process, which has a structured theology, with groups like the Divine Light Mission or the Children of God, where members base their commitment almost entirely upon experiences. Whether the experience was called Knowledge or baptism in the Holy Spirit, it was beyond description. Such experience-oriented groups find talk an inferior method of communication at best.

But I had not shared the experience with any with any of these other groups. I am also partial to talking. The Process had not given up on the mind. The members did not regard thought as an enemy. As a result I found them more consistently interesting than any of the other groups that I encountered.

Many groups, particularly the Jesus People, attract a high percentage of ex-addicts and other casualties of modern society who delight in confessing their past sins to visitors. The Process too has its ex-addicts. In Toronto I met a young Process Messenger who told me how she had been on drugs for years before meeting up with the Process. But most of those I met had no such horror stories to tell about their past lives. Process publicity stresses that while the church helps individuals in trouble, it does not help them so that it can convert them. The ex-addict told me that no one ever tried to get her to join the Process. She just kept coming to the coffee house because she felt drawn to it, and finally asked to join.

There is a great deal to be said for groups, like many among the Jesus People, which offer a haven for the walking wounded of the late twentieth century. But one does not need to be at the bottom, physically, emotionally and spiritually, to join the Process. Simply getting into the Process or the Foundation in a formal way requires a fair amount of self-control and moving up in the hierarchy is hard work. Personal responsibility, they say, is at the core of their beliefs and resultant lifestyle. The group certainly offers no promise of instant salvation or instant peace upon joining.

But that observation leads to an important, perhaps basic question about the group. Why would people who were apparently making it in the outside world already want to join up in the first place? Mother Mercedes said that she joined after she saw the change the Process had brought about in her own brother. Brother Amos said he was attracted by the control and sense of purpose that Processeans radiated. Father Joab said he liked the doctrines. No one seemed to have undergone a particularly intense emotional experience upon joining.

I confess that this has left me with a rather uncomfortable feeling that there is something very important about the Process that I am missing. Process or Foundation theology, as I understand it, is not particularly original. There are plenty of apocalyptic sects around. A meeting with Robert de Grimston might have made things clearer to me. Often a charismatic leader can attract a group of highly talented followers through the exercise of his own magnetic personality.

In the end, though, I will accept the Process or Foundation at its own evaluation, as a small group of dedicated individuals earnestly trying to find a way of reaching a state of detachment, invulnerability, and dignity in the face of a worldwide doom which they feel is inevitable and very near at hand.

Conclusion

As we said at the very beginning of the book, religious diversity was one of the principles upon which America was founded. And as we have seen, religious diversity is still very much a part of the American scene today, perhaps more now than ever before.

The very diversity of today's popular new religions makes one hesitant about drawing any grand sweeping conclusions about them or their future. But a few final thoughts and suggestions might prove useful.

The first suggestion is, don't panic. In discussing groups like the Children of God or the witchcraft covens, particularly with parents, one senses a real feeling of fear. Some of the recently published criticisms of Eastern and occult groups have been downright hysterical. The source of the fear is an underlying belief that these groups really do have some sort of special power, hypnotic, demmonic or whatever.

Some parents feel that their perfectly normal and happy children will suddenly and mysteriously be sucked in and entraped by strange doctrines. Some unorthodox religious groups encourage this sort of fear by stressing how people joined after suddenly "seeing the light," that is, undergoing a miraculous and instantaneous conversion.

My interviews with members of a variety of unorthodox religious groups in no way support the theory of instant conversion. Committing oneself to an unorthodox religion is almost always just another step in a long process of seeking alternatives to what might be called "the American way of life."

The vast majority of those who have joined unorthodox religions were dissatisfied with the lives they were leading, unhappy—often desperately unhappy—about what the future seemed to hold for them. The conversion might look rapid, but it was a long time in coming.

All of these groups, even the grimmest, gloomiest and most apocalyptic of them, are really optimistic. In writing about British cults, Dr. Christopher Evans concluded that the basic message of these groups was "Man . . . does have a future, and a future far better, far clearer than the one predicted by orthodox politicians, clergymen and technocrats." The same could certainly be said about the unorthodox religions in America.

They may preach impending doom for most of the world, but they expect to survive the catastrophe, because they are on God's side. They may demand rigid discipline, poverty, even a degree of mortification of the flesh, but they promise and often deliver a feeling of inner serenity, of being at peace with the world.

These unorthodox religions have answers to questions about the universe and man's purpose in life and what happens after death. These are questions for which society at large can no longer provide convincing answers.

There is nothing mysterious about the appeal of a group which can offer individuals a measure of serenity and happiness, and the feeling that the universe makes sense.

That's part of the explanation for the appeal of the unorthodox religions, but only part. After all, there were plenty of unorthodox religions before the development of the atom bomb made us suspect that man might be an endangered species. There were plenty even before Charles Darwin dropped his own bomb over a century ago and blasted man out of his special place at the apex of creation. There have always, it seems, been a certain percentage of people who have desired a deeper or different sort of religious experience. Perhaps that percentage is about the same now that it has always been, and only the forms of religious commitment have changed.

So, as I said, don't panic. No strange new forces have been let loose on the land.

Having said that, I would also like to warn against any attempt to sweep the whole phenomena of unorthodox religion aside as "youthful foolishness" or cover it with some other equally insulting and empty phrase. I think that it would be extremely difficult for anyone to talk to as many of the new believers as I have and not be deeply impressed by their seriousness and their genuine willingness to sacrifice for their beliefs. We may not agree with the way in which they have chosen to confront the problems of this life, but we can't pass it off as a lark.

What of the future? I'm really no better at prophecy than anyone else, but as we have said, the current religious situation is not an entirely unique one, so past history may provide some guide to the future.

Most of the groups we have discussed have formed around a single powerful figure, David Berg, Sun Myung Moon, Guru Maharaj Ji, Prabhupada, Robert de Grimston. When this figure dies, or is otherwise removed from the scene, as has already happened in the case of the Foundation, the group is in great peril. The vast majority of religious movements do not long outlive their founder. Only if they have developed a strong secondary leadership and an efficient structure can they survive.

Apocalyptic religions will have to learn to come to terms with a world that will not end. It's been done before. The early Christians certainly thought the world was going to come to an end within their lifetime, yet the world survived for nearly two thousand years and so did Christianity.

Most of the new believers feel they must confront the problem of how they are going to change the world. But the world has proved remarkably resistant to change, at least to any organized or planned change. The Age of Aquarius is as unlikely as the apocalypse. The real problem confronted by most of these groups, I think, is not how they are going to change the world, but how they are going to keep the world from changing them.

For Further Information

Anyone desiring further information about the groups mentioned in this book may wish to contact them directly. If you live in a major metropolitain area the best thing to do is look in the telephone book. The larger religious groups have centers in many of the major cities. Unorthodox religions are particularly well-represented in areas like New York, Chicago and Los Angeles, but they can be found other places as well. There is, for example, a Hare Krishna center in Pittsburgh. Denver is not only the center for the Divine Light Mission in America, it is also where the Guru Maharaj Ji lives when he is in this country. Minneapolis is a hotbed of witchcraft. Unorthodox religion, therefore, is not only a product of southern California and New York; Middle America has its share.

What follows is a list of addresses that I hope you will find useful. Remember, though, that these groups change locations frequently, and occasionally even change their names, so some of the addresses on this list may no longer be valid.

Children of God colonies are constantly on the move, but the group has maintained a fairly stable central mailing address. It is: Box 119, Dallas, Texas 75221.

The rest of the Jesus movement is so fragmented that there are no central addresses. Many of the communes are wary of publicity and would not like to have their addresses published anyway. The best source for up-to-date information on the movement is one of the Jesus newspapers. These used to be published in profusion, but their popularity appears to have diminished considerably. The largest of the papers is the *Hollywood Free Paper*.

The Charismatic Renewal Movement likewise has no single national center, though centers can be found at many universities, particularly Catholic universities. The most active Charismatic center in my area was at St. Francis Seminary, Lafayette, New Jersey 07848. In New York City, the address of the Unification Church is 475 Fifth Avenue, New York, New York 10017.

The Eastern religions are more centrally organized. The main address for the Divine Light Mission is 511 East 16th Street, Box 6495, Denver, Colorado 80206. For Hare Krishna, write International Society for Krishna Consciousness, 3764 Wateska Avenue, Los Angeles, California 90034. The Maharishi's doctrine is taught in so many centers that you should try your telephone book first. Maharishi International University recently purchased the campus of Parsons College in Fairfield, Iowa, and you can address a letter to them there: Maharishi International University, Fairfield, Iowa 52556. In New York City, the Maharishi International University is located at 59 West 46th Street, New York, New York 10036. Subud can be reached through Box 553, Old Chelsea Station, New York, New York 10011.

Both Dr. Leo Louis Martello, Suite 1B, 153 West 80th Street, New York, New York 10024, and Gavin Frost of the School of Wicca, Route 2, Salem, Missouri 65560, sell Witchcraft courses. Dr. Martello will answer queries only if accompanied by a self-addressed stamped envelope. A good source of Witchcraft information is *Gnostica News,* Box 3383, St. Paul, Minnesota 55165.

The Church of Satan in San Francisco, California, lists only a telephone number: (415) 752-3583.

The Eastern headquarters of the Foundation is 111 East 38th Street, New York, New York 10016.

Bibliography

ANDREWS, EDWARD DEMING. *The People Called Shakers*. New York: Dover, 1963.

BLESSITT, ARTHUR, with WAGER, WALTER. *Turned on to Jesus*. New York: Hawthorn, 1971.

BRADEN, CHARLES S. *These Also Believe*. New York: Macmillan, 1949.

BUCKLAND, RAYMOND. *Witchcraft from the Inside*. St. Paul, Minn.: Llewellyn Publishing, 1971.

CLARK, STEPHEN B. *Baptized in the Spirit*. Pecos, N.M.: Dove Publications, 1970.

COHEN, DANIEL. *Masters of the Occult*. New York: Dodd, Mead, 1971.

————. *Not of the World*. Chicago: Follett, 1973.

————. *Voodoo, Devils and the New Invisible World*. New York: Dodd, Mead, 1972.

COHN, NORMAN. *The Pursuit of the Millennium*. Fairlawn, N.J.: Essential Books, 1959.

EBON, MARTIN, ed. *Witchcraft Today.* New York: New American Library, 1971.

ENROTH, RONALD M., ERICSON, EDWARD E., JR., and PETERS, C. BRECK-ENRIDGE. *The Jesus People.* Grand Rapids, Mich.: Eerdmans, 1972.

EVANS, CHRISTOPHER. *Cults of Unreason.* New York: Farrar, Straus and Giroux, 1973.

GARDNER, GERALD. *Witchcraft Today.* London: Jarrolds, 1968.

HEENAN, EDWARD F., ed. *Mystery, Magic and Miracle.* Englewood Cliffs, N.J.: Prentice-Hall, 1973.

HEMBREE, CHARLES R. *Fruits of the Spirit.* Grand Rapids, Mich.: Baker Book House, 1971.

HOLZER, HANS. *The Truth About Witchcraft.* New York: Doubleday, 1969.

HUGHES, PENNETHORNE. *Witchcraft.* Baltimore: Penguin, 1967.

JAMES, WILLIAM. *The Varieties of Religious Experience.* New York: Collier Books, 1961.

LA VEY, ANTON S. *The Satanic Bible.* New York: Avon, 1969.

LYONS, ARTHUR. *The Second Coming: Satanism in America.* New York: Dodd, Mead, 1970.

MALKO, GEORGE. *Scientiology—The Now Religion.* New York: Delacorte, 1970.

MATHISON, RICHARD. *God is a Millionaire.* New York: Charter Books, 1962.

MC FADDEN, MICHAEL. *The Jesus Revolution.* New York: Harper, 1972.

MC LOUGHLIN, WILLIAM, and BELLAH, ROBERT, eds. *Religion in America.* New York: Beacon, 1968.

MELVILLE, KEITH. *Communes in the Counter Culture.* New York: Morrow, 1972.

MICHELMORE, PETER. *Back to Jesus.* New York: Fawcett, 1973.

MOODY, JESS. *The Jesus Freaks.* Waco, Texas: Word Books, 1972.

MORRIS, JAMES. *The Preachers.* New York: St. Martins, 1973.

MURRAY, MARGARET. *The Witch Cult in Western Europe.* London: Oxford, 1921.

NEEDLEMAN, JACOB. *The New Religions.* New York: Doubleday, 1970.

RANAGHAN, KEVIN and DOROTHY. *Catholic Pentecostals.* New York: Paulist Press, 1969.

RHODES, H.T.F. *The Satanic Mass.* London: Rider, 1954.

ROWLEY, PETER. *New Gods in America.* New York: McKay, 1971.

SAMARIN, WILLIAM J. *Tongues of Men and Angels.* New York: Macmillan, 1972.

SMITH, SUSY. *Today's Witches.* Englewood Cliffs, N.J.: Prentice-Hall, 1970.

SNOOK, JOHN B. *Going Further: Life-and-Death Religion in America.* Englewood Cliffs, N.J.: Prentice-Hall, 1973.

SYMONDS, JOHN. *The Great Beast.* London: Rider, 1951.

WATTS, ALAN. *Beyond Theology.* New York: Random House, 1964.

Who is Guru Maharaj Ji? New York: Bantam, 1973.

Index

Acts, Book of, 12
Adam and Eve, Reverend Moon on, 66
Age of Aquarius, 91
  witchcraft and, 135
Alamo, Susan, 45-49
Alamo, Tony, 45-49
Alcohol (drinking),
  Christian Foundation and, 46
  Hare Krishnas and, 111
  Process and, 164
All Worlds, Church of, 144
American Foundation for the Science
  of Creative Intelligence. 96
Amos (prophet), 145
Amos, Brother, 163, 164, 174
And It Is Divine, 92
Animals,
  Church of Satan and, 155
  Process and, 172-73
Antinomians, Children of God and, 22-
  23
Apocalyptic religions, 13, 177. *See also*
  Children of God; Process
Aquarian age, 91
  witchcraft and, 135
Arabs. *See* Middle East
Aradia, or Gospel of the Witches,
  133-34
Astrodome (Houston), Guru Maharaj
  Ji's Millennium '73, 78, 80-81, 90-
  92, 115
Augustine, St., 146

Back to Godhead, 109
Back to Jesus, 44
Bal Bhagwan Ji, 91
Bapak, 119ff.

Baptism,
  in the Holy Spirit, Charismatic Re-
    newal and, 58
  mass, 47
Bartok, Eva, 117-18
Beatles, the, 96, 98
Berg, David, 23-25ff., 36ff.
Berg, Virginia Brandt, 23
Bhagavad-Gita, 82-83
Bhole Ji, 91, 92
Bible. *See also* Christianity; Jesus
  Christ; specific Books
  Children of God and, 22, 36, 38
  Christian Foundation and, 48
  Jesus People and, 43, 48
  Process and prophecy in, 164
Bibliography, 183-85
Black masses, 130, 152
Black Muslims, 15-16
Blavatsky, Madame, 13, 14
Blessitt, Arthur, 44
Blue Aquarius, 91, 92
Bonewits, P. E. I., 137, 139, 149-50,
  154, 156
Book of Shadows, 131
"Brainwashing," Children of God and,
  34-35
British, the. *See* England
Buddha, Divine Light Mission and, 80

California. *See also* specific cities.
  Children of God in, 23-25
  Christian Foundation in, 46-49
  Jesus People in, 42. *See also* Children
    of God; Christian Foundation
  Satanism in, 156
Campbell, Colin, 104

Catholic Pentecostals, 58
Catholics,
  and Charismatic Renewal, 53-62
  as Children of God, 31
  and the Devil, 147
Cayce, Edgar, 164
Central Park (New York), witchcraft
  ritual in, 129
Chanting, 112-13. *See also* Hare Krish-
  nas
Charismatic Renewal, 53-62
  how to contact, 180
Children,
  Children of God and, 38-39
  Church of Satan and, 155
  Hare Krishnas and. *See* Hare Krish-
  nas
  Process and, 163
Children of God (COGs), 21-40, 42, 45
  address, 180
  Process and, 161
Christ. *See* Jesus Christ
Christ Commune (pseudonym), 49-52
Christian Foundation, 45-49
Christian Science, 12-13
Christianity (Christians). *See also*
  Catholics
  new, 21-73. *See also* Charismatic Re-
  newal; Children of God; Jesus
  People; Unification Church
  and Satanism, 130-31, 145-47ff.
  and witchcraft, 137, 138
Church of Satan. *See* Satan, Church of
Cloud of Unknowing, The, 97-98
Coffee houses,
  Christian, 23-24
  Process, 168
Colorado. *See also* Denver
  Guru Maharaj Ji in, 78
Communes; communal living, 12, 49-
  52. *See also* specific groups
Cooper, Julie, 79, 80, 83, 84, 86, 89, 92
Council of American Witches, 142
Crowley, Aleister, 144, 148, 153
Cults of Unreason, 112-13

Dallas,
  Children of God address in, 180
  Explo '72, 41, 42
  Hare Krishnas, 108, 112
Dancing,
  Children of God and, 37, 39
  Christian Foundation and, 46
  Hare Krishnas and, 105-6, 107, 112
  witchcraft ritual, 140-41
Darwin, Charles, 177
Das, Prajapati, 111-12

Daughters of the American Revolution,
  128
Davis, Franklin M., 103
Davis, Rennie, 78-79, 92
De Grimston, Mary Ann, 167
De Grimston, Robert, 161, 166ff.,
  170ff., 174
Demeter (goddess), 130
Denver, Divine Light Mission in, 179
"Deprogramming," 33
Devil. *See* Satan; Satanism
Dirksen, Everett, 22
Divine Light Mission, 77-94, 179
  address of, 180
Dixon, Jean, 164
Drinking. *See* Alcohol
Drugs (drug addicts),
  Christ Commune and, 50
  Christian Foundation and, 46
  Hare Krishnas and, 111
  Process and, 164, 174
  Satanism and, 149-50, 154, 156
  and witchcraft, 141-42
Druids, 144
Duquesne University, 56

"Earthquake fever," 24-25
Eastern religions, 15, 75-123. *See also*
  Divine Light Mission; Hare Krish-
  nas; Subud; Transcendental Medi-
  tation
Eddy, Mary Baker, 12-13, 93
El Paso Herald Post, 32
England (the British), 176
  Druidic group, 144
  Hellfire Club, 147-48
  and the Process, 167
  and witchcraft, 137
Enroth, Ronald M., 26-27, 43. *See also*
  Jesus People, The
Ericson, Edward E., Jr., 26-27, 43. *See*
  also Jesus People, The
Europe, Children of God in, 28
Evans, Christopher, 113, 176
Exit (de Grimston), 170
Exorcist, The, 130, 148
Explo '72, 41, 42

Fairfield, Iowa, Maharishi International
  University address in, 180
Fakiranand, Mahatma, 89-90
Farrow, Mia, 96
Fisherman's Wharf (San Francisco),
  witch's museum at, 138
Flavin, Robert, 160
Fleetwood, Susan. *See* Alamo, Susan
Fletcher, Richard, 89

Food,
Hare Krishna meals, 111
Process and, 171
Foundation, the, 16, 158-74
address for, 181
Franklin, Benjamin, and the Hellfire Club, 148
Free love. *See* Sex
FREECOG, 32-33
Frisbee, Lonnie, 43
Frost, Gavin, 134-35, 138, 139-40ff.
address of, 180
Frost, Yvonne, 134

Gaddafi, Mu'ammar, 28-30
Gambling, Hare Krishnas and, 111
Gardner, Gerald, 137-38, 144
Garrison, N.Y., Charismatic Renewal gathering at, 57
Glossolalia, Charismatic Renewal and, 54-55, 56-57, 58-61
Gnostica News, 139, 142, 180
Gnostics, 146
Golden Dawn, 144
Gosvami, Hrdayananda Dasa, 115-16
Graham, Billy, 44
and Astrodome, 90
and Explo '72, 41, 42
and witchcraft, 128
Graves, Robert, 137, 144
Green Egg, The, 144
Guru Maharaj Ji, 12, 77-94, 179
Hare Krishnas and, 115

Halley, Pat, 89
Harder, Mary White, 49
Hare Krishnas, 105-16, 179
how to contact, 180
Harrison, George, 96
Healing,
Charismatic Renewal and, 55, 56-57, 59
Process and, 171
witchcraft and, 132
Heinlein, Robert, 144
Hellfire Club, 147-48
Herberg, Will, 23
Hershfield, Howard, 86-87
Hindu religion. *See also* Hare Krishnas and Theosophy, 13
Hippies. *See* Jesus People
Hitler, Adolf, kept from invading England by witchcraft, 137
Hoffman, Abbie, 79
Hoffman, Bernard. *See* Alamo, Tony
Hollywood Free Paper, 180
Holy Land. *See* Israel

Holy Rollers. *See* Pentecostalism
Houston, Guru Maharaj Ji in, 78, 80-81, 90-92, 115
Hrdayananda dasa Gosvami, 115-16
Hubbard, L. Ron., 15
Huntington Beach, Calif., 23-24

India. *See also* Divine Light Mission; Hare Krishnas; Transcendental Meditation
Vedas and, 14
Indonesia. *See* Subud
International Meditation Society (IMS), 96
International Society for Krishna Consciousness (ISKCON). *See* Hare Krishnas
Isle of Man, 138
Israel,
Children of God and, 28ff.
Jesus People and, 43
Italy, witchcraft in, 130

Japan(ese), 15
Unification Church and, 65, 68, 70
Jehovah, Process and, 159, 162
Jehovah's Witnesses, 13
Jesus Christ, 116
Children of God quote, 36
Divine Light Mission and, 80
Process and, 159, 161
Reverend Moon, Unification Church and, 66
Jesus Peace, 61-62
Jesus People, 41-52, 86, 173, 174. *See also* Children of God
Hare Krishnas and, 115
how to contact, 180
and Process, 161
and witchcraft, 127-28
Jesus People, The, 26-27, 43, 45
Jewishness, Process and, 162
Jews. *See also* Judeo-Christian tradition
Children of God and, 30, 35
Reverend Moon on Jesus and, 66
Ji, Guru Maharaj. *See* Guru Maharaj Ji
Joan of Arc, as witch, 136
Joab, Father, 160ff., 167, 171
Johnson, Marilyn Lois, 93
Jordan, Fred, 23, 25-26, 34-35
Judeo-Christian tradition, and witchcraft, 137, 138

Karma, witchcraft and, 129, 132
Kelly, Aidan, 140-41, 144
Kelly, Ken, 85, 88-89
Kinsolving, Lester, 113

Kohoutek (comet), Children of God and, 21, 31
Divine Light Mission and, 91
Korea(ns), and Reverend Moon, Unification Church, 64-65ff.
Krassner, Paul, 79
Krishna; Krishna Consciousness. *See* Hare Krishnas

Lafayette, N. J., Charismatic Renewal address in, 180
Latihan, 118ff.
LaVey, Anton Szandor, 150-56
LaVey, Diane, 152
Lefland, John, 71-72, 73
Leland, C. G., 133-34
Libya, Children of God and, 28
Lord of the Rings, 144
Los Angeles,
    Children of God and, 25, 29
    Hare Krishna address in, 180
    Jesus People and Sunset Strip, 42, 44
    Transcendental Meditation in, 97
Lucifer, Process and, 159
Lyons, Arthur, 152, 157, 163

Madison Square Garden (New York), Reverend Sun Myung Moon in, 63-64, 67-68, 69-70
Magic. *See* Satanism; Witchcraft
Maharishi International University (MIU), 96-97, 101
    address, 180
Maharishi Mahesh Yogi, 95-104
    contacting, 180
Manichaeism, 146
Mansfield, Jayne, and Church of Satan, 150
Manson, Charles, 156, 157
    and Process, 160
Mantras, for Transcendental Meditation, 97-98ff.
Marriage,
    Children of God and, 38
    Christ Commune and, 51
    Hare Krishnas and, 110-11
    Process and, 163
    Unification Church and, 66-67
    witchcraft and, 141
Martello, Leo Louis, 129, 131, 139
    address of, 180
Masons, rite of, 142
Massachusetts,
    Puritans in, 12
    witchcraft trials in Salem, 128
Meditation, 97-104. *See also* specific groups

Mercedes, Mother, 164, 167-68, 169, 171, 174
Process and, 162
Unification Church and, 66, 72-73
Mexico, Children of God in, 28
Micah, Father, 161-62
Michelmore, Peter, 44
Michigan, University of, 61
Michigan State University, 61
Middle East, Children of God and, 28-31
Millennium '73 (Houston), 78, 80-81, 90-92, 115
Miller, William, 13
Minneapolis, witchcraft in, 179
Moon, Sun Myung, 63-73
Moor, Robert de Grimston. *See* De Grimston, Robert
Moore, Paul, 66
Mormons, 12, 13
Moses David. *See* Berg, David
Murder (human sacrifice), and Satanism, 149-50, 154-55, 156
Murray, Margaret, 136-37

Napoleon, witchcraft and, 137
NBC, and Children of God, 32, 33
Needleman, Jacob, 121, 122
Neo-Paganism, 144
New Jersey. *See also* specific places
    Charismatic Renewal in, 54-55
New Reformed Orthodox Order of the Golden Dawn, 144
New Religions, The (Needleman), 121, 122
New York City,
    Children of God in, 21, 31
    Divine Light Mission in, 93
    Hare Krishnas in, 107-8, 111, 115
    Jesus People in, 44
    Maharishi International University address in, 180
    Process (Foundation) in, 170, 172, 181
    Subud address in, 180
    Unification Church, Reverend Sun Myung Moon in, 63-64, 67-68, 69-70, 180
    witchcraft in, 129, 180
New York Dolls, 164
New York Post, and Process, 161, 168
New York State. *See* specific places
New York Times,
    and Charismatic Renewal, 62
    and Hare Krishnas, 111-12, 114
    and Unification Church, Reverend Moon, 64, 66, 70

New York Times Magazine, on Guru
    Maharaj Ji, 91
Nixon, Richard, Reverend Moon and,
    65
Nostradamus, 164
Notre Dame University, 61
Noyes, John Humphrey, 12
Nudity,
    and Satanic ritual, 152
    witchcraft and, 133-34, 140-41

Occult, the, 125-74. *See also* Process
    (Foundation); Satanism; Witch-
    craft
Olcott, William P., 13
Oneida community, 12
Opinion Research Center of Chicago,
    149
Otis, Leon S., 101, 102

Paganism, 143-44. *See also* Witchcraft
Pak, Bo Hi, 71
Park, Chung Hee, 71
Patrick, Ted, 33
Paul VI, and the Devil, 148
Pennsylvania. *See also* specific places
    Quakers, 12
Pentecostalism, 56-58, 61
Persephone (goddess), 130
Peters, C. Breckenridge, 26-27, 43. *See
    also Jesus People, The*
Pittsburgh,
    Charismatic Renewal in, 56, 58
    Hare Krishnas in, 179
Polanski, Roman, 156
Prabhupada, A. C. Bhaktivedenta
    Swami, 107-8, 109, 111ff.
Process (Foundation), 16, 158-74
    address, 181
Protestant-Catholic-Jew (Herberg), 23
Protestants. *See also* Pentecostalism
    and the Devil, 147
Psychology Today, 104
Puritans, 12

Qaddafi, Muammar el-, 28-30
Quakers, 12

Ranaghan, Kevin and Dorothy, 56, 58,
    61
Ray, John, 135, 139, 142
Reincarnation, witchcraft and, 129, 141
Revolutionaries for Jesus. *See* Children
    of God
Rhea, Mother, 165
Richardson, James T., 49
Roman Catholics. *See* Catholics
Rosemary's Baby, 130, 148, 150, 156

Sade, Marquis de, 147
St. Francis Seminary, 180
St. Paul, Minn., witch meeting in, 139
Salem, Mass., witchcraft trials in, 128
Salem, Mo., witchcraft in, 135
    address, 180
Samarin, William J., 59, 60-61
San Francisco,
    Jesus People in, 42
    Satanism in, 150-56, 181
    witchcraft museum in, 138
Satan. *See also* Satanism
    Process and, 159ff.
    Unification Church and, 66, 71-72, 73
Satan, Church of, 150-56
    phone number of, 181
Satanic Bible, 150, 153
Satanism, 145-57
    Process and. *See* Process
    vs. witchcraft, 130-31
Satsang, 83-84ff.
Schwartz, Gary, 102-3
Science (magazine), 100
*Science of Being and Art of Living,
    The,* 96
Scientology, Church of, 15
Sex (sexual relations). *See aslo* Mar-
    riage
    Children of God and, 33, 38
    Christ Commune and, 51
    Hare Krishnas and, 110-11
    Oneida community and, 12
    Process and, 163-64
    Satanism and, 148
    Shakers and, 12
    Unification Church, Reverend Moon,
        and, 64, 67
    witchcraft and, 141
Shakers, 12
Sharron, Mark, 88
Shri Hans Ji Maharaj, 80
Shri Mata Ji, 80
Sicily, witchcraft in, 130
Simmonds, Robert B., 49
Singing and songs,
    Children of God and, 37, 39
    Christian Foundation hymns, 48
Sino-Japanese religions, 15
Sirhan, Sirhan, 156
Smith, Hershel, 127
Smith, Joseph, 12, 93
Smoking,
    Christian Foundation and, 46
    Process and, 171
Snook, John B., 62
Sonny and Cher, 45
Speaking in tongues, Charismatic Re-
    newal and, 54-55, 56-57, 58-61

Spiritual Regeneration Movement (SRM), 96
Spiritual Sky Scented Products Company, 108
Spiritualism, 13
Stanford Research Institute, 101-2
Stonehenge, 144
Stranger in a Strange Land, 144
Students' International Meditation Society (SIMS), 96
Subud, 117-23
address, 180
Subuh, Muhammad (Bapak), 119ff.

Tarrytown, N.Y., Unification Church estate in, 67, 70
Tate, Sharon, 156
Teens for Christ. *See* Children of God
Telepathy, Process and, 171
Texas. *See also* specific cities
Children of God in, 25
Theosophy, 13-14
Time (magazine),
on Church of Satan, 154
on witchcraft ritual, 140-41
Tolkien, J. R. R., 144
Tongues of Men and Angels (Samarin), 59, 60-61
Toronto, Canada, Process Church in, 158-59, 173
Transcendental Meditation (TM), 95-104
how to contact Maharishi Mahesh Yogi, 180

Ultimate Sin, The, 172
Unification Church, 63-73
contacting, 180
United Nations, Children of God demonstrate at, 21, 31

Vedata Society, 14
Vedas,
and Hare Krishna, 106

Vedanta Society, 14
Venta, Krishna, 113
Vivekananda, Swami, 14

Wales; the Welsh, and witchcraft, 134, 141
Wallace, George, 154
Wallace, Robert Keith, 100, 101
Washington, D. C., Unification Church demonstrates in, 65
White Goddess, The, 137
Wicca, Church of, 135
Williams, Robert J., 129
Williamson, Cecil, 138
Willowbrook, 160
Wilmington, Del., mass baptism in, 47
Witchcraft, 127-44, 179
addresses of interest, 180
Witches Anti-Defamation League, 129
Witches International Craft Associates (WICA), 131
Witches Liberation Movement, 129, 131
Witches Trine, The, 144
Witch's Mill and Kitchen Museum, 138
Women. *See also* Sex
Children of God and, 38
Christ Commune and, 50-51
Christian Foundation and, 46
Hare Krishna and, 110
Process and, 172
and witchcraft, 130, 140, 141
Women's International Terrorist Corps from Hell (WITCH), 140
World War II, witchcraft in, 137

Yogis. *See also* Maharishi Mahesh Yogi
scientific studies of, 98-100

Zell, Tim, 144
Zen, 16
scientific study of, 98-100